Always Kristen

A Memoir

What readers are saying....

It arrived yesterday, and I couldn't put it down today until I finished it. Wonderful read that shows us a mother's love has no limits. This book had me in tears numerous times.

I received this book in the mail Saturday and started reading it Sunday. Couldn't put it down except when I was crying. Finished it in one day. What a heartbreaking and also a heartwarming story. Praying for these 2 beautiful women as they continue on their journey. Much Love and God Bless. This is a must read book!

This a remarkable story that brought me to tears more than once. The unconditional love of a mother for her transgender child and the heart wrenching, emotionally charged twists and turns of their lives. It is a must read.

The courageous journey of a transgender child written by the devoted mother who took that journey with her. Nelson writes with both honesty and sensitivity as she describes moments of frustration and despair, challenges and triumphs, as Kristen grows into her new identity and her family's love and acceptance grows along with her. In the end, it is the story of the love between a mother and a child who is "different", and how hope is born out of the love that cherishes those differences.

Totally recommend this book to everyone to read. The reader will garner information into the life of a person who has dealt with too much dilemma that most of us won't understand. This book provides insight into a family that has shared its most intimate experiences.

I just finished the book and was so overwhelmed with the emotions that the writing evoked. Surely it will be helpful to others who are navigating this same path- as with all new areas there is no roadmap. As a retired bereavement counselor, I was reminded of one of the things we often discussed in bereavement group - that kindness and compassion are so important as we never know when we meet someone what burden they bear. Great read for families struggling with transgender issues in this culture.

"In a mom's concrete and hit-the-ground-running examination of what parenting means once we understand that it's not controlling the lives of our children, Rita Nelson allows us to watch her discovery of the fullness of the life she brought into the world. I closed the book grateful for this humane and clear-eyed treatment of an issue too often reduced to sound bites."

—Barbara Cawthorne Crafton,
Episcopal Priest, Spiritual Director, and Author

"When I first started reading this book I could not put it down. I felt that the author was writing about me. The names were changed and locations different but Kristen and I had so much in common I had to find out what was going to happen to me. It was after meeting with my mother, Rita and Kristen that I was able to inform my father of my life long dreams and aspirations."

—Kathy Carpenter,
Miss Sussex County

"Always Kristen is a story of exploration, determination, and bravery. What comes through on every page is a mother's fierce love for her child that cannot help but touch your own heart."

—Ellen Collins,
author of *The Memory Thief*

Published by:
Empyrean Publishing

30895 Crepe Myrtle Drive

Suite 66

Millsboro, DE 19966

ISBN-13: 978-1544197821

ISBN-10: 1544197829

Library of Congress Card Number: 2017903400

The names of some people have been changed to protect their privacy.

Always Kristen

A Memoir

A mother's journey from

"It's a boy" to "Mom, I'm a Girl."

By

Rita B. Nelson

This book is dedicated

To

My beautiful daughter, Kristen, who has the courage to be true to herself, and from whom I learned so much about her, about transgender people, and about myself as we walked together on this journey,

and

To all the families who have a transgender child and who open their minds and hearts in acceptance and love,

and

To my husband, whose love, patience, support, and encouragement have sustained me for the seemingly endless years it took me to write this book.

CONTENTS

Prologue....1
Somewhere in the Middle....3
Early Signs....15
And on Top of All That....33
Good Lord, Deliver Us....53
What Next?....65
One Piece of the Puzzle....73
Annie....99
The Bahama Mama....107
Fast Forward....117
Secrets....125
A Celebration of Life....133
Pronouns and Names....139
All in The Family....143
A World Unraveled…....151
Good Intentions....165
Coming Home....181
Finding Kristen....189
No Going Back....203
Being a Girl....211

The Artiste 217
Change...225
Limbo 233
Epilogue...243
Acknowledgments...247
About the Author 249

PROLOGUE

They say there is a book inside every person. Inside of me is a book about my son, Christopher. As I began writing it, I realized it was more about myself than it was about him, but writing about myself or my feelings is one of the most difficult things for me to do. The exposure to a whole host of people, even strangers, frightens me. It renders me vulnerable in a way I have never experienced. However, more often my feelings are the real heart of my life with a unique, bright, out-of-the-ordinary child.

From the earliest stirrings of Christopher in utero, I had a mother's intuition that this was not going to be any run-of-the-mill child. Oh, no. Even as he grew from the seed of life, his restless moving, kicking and turning were extraordinary, struggling, it seemed, to be born, to become. It is a struggle that continues to this day.

Christopher is a male to female transgender child. Learning this, digesting this, accepting this, loving my child, is a journey I had never expected to take. Shoving my fear aside, I now share my life with this child with you, my readers.

What follows is what I hope is an honest, heartfelt story of my life with my second child who, to this day, is an unnatural priority in my life, even, at times, above my extremely deep love for my second husband, William. Since he is not Christopher's biological father, I thank God every day he has even a modicum of understanding in this regard, for a lesser man would have fled my life years ago. Why one child becomes so wrapped around one's heart is a depth I cannot fathom, but I know it is true.

It seems so futile to think about starting this book with "Once upon a time," when there is no certainty that there will, or can be, a "happily ever after," although that is every mother's dream for her children. So many memories and feelings consume me from day to day whenever I stop and really think about my second child that the place to begin could be almost anywhere. Books starting at the beginning sometimes drag along and bore me – "Let's get to the good stuff." Books starting at the end take out much of the mystery on the story's journey backward. Starting in the middle may be the best right now since there is no end, only acceptance, and the tale to be woven with the threads and strands of my child's forty plus years of life.

Rita B. Nelson
Rosedale Beach, Delaware
2017

SOMEWHERE IN THE MIDDLE

Here in the middle of the muddle of life, I am sitting at my desk in a corner of our second- floor loft. My desk is by a bay window overlooking one large, hourglass-shaped pond straddled at its narrow neck by a large white gazebo. The sun is streaming in from the large skylight. Behind me is my fifteen-foot long bookcase with all my cherished books. They somehow give me comfort, like my old, worn teddy bear long since lost amid one move or another. I love every one of them. It is quiet. The only living thing around is my white fluff ball of a four-pound Maltese. He is sleeping in his bed just behind me, my ever-present sentinel.

My desk is cluttered with pens, pencils, receipts that need to be entered into the computer, a day-old cup of tea, genealogy reports on a friend's relative I am researching, and the blank screen of my computer, luring me into its emptiness, begging me to fill it up with my wounded heart's story.

I am trying to write about my life with my transgender daughter, and I thought what I was going to write would be about her. But it is not, I find. It is about me too. And while I can splash many things about me onto that screen, the deep inner feelings, sometimes even dark ones I feel about my daughter, get stuck in my throat and I am unable to fling them onto that blank page staring back at me. I sit there in quiet contemplation, tears of some emotion I have not yet identified falling on my lap.

Okay, time for me to find that rag of courage and wipe away my tears. I look out the window at the cascading fountain in the middle of the pond, forever recycling the water from below, tossing it up, up high, before bursting into a thousand shimmering droplets, gathering in life-giving oxygen before they return to the rippling pond, only to repeat the cycle again and again and again. My life is like that, I think. I am but a droplet in the fountain of life. I have only one cycle of time in which to reach to the stars, gather life, and tell my story before I fall into my eternity.

Enough musing. I'll gather some droplets from the pond of my heart and toss my feelings up high and out onto that blank page for others to read, to feel, to travel with me on my journey with my special, unique, frustrating, loveable daughter, who, while born Christopher, has always been Kristen. I've stalled long enough. I'll start by throwing the who of my daughter on this page, I say. Maybe, that will help open me up, allow me to be vulnerable enough to write about the who that I am as her mother and how I feel about her. Maybe.

She is so complex. I'll start with her beauty. Beauty in her infectious, melodious laugh, her blonde, lion-like mane, the twinkle in her light umber eyes. Beauty in the patience she shows answering the endless questions of our four-year-old neighbor. Beauty in her inventiveness assembling an easel from scrap metal. Beauty in her willingness to help others, like feeding our neighbor's kittens while they are on vacation or opening our neighbor's unit to accept delivery of his oxygen for his next visit. Beauty in her intelligence that awes me as she explains a black hole to me or tries to get me to understand the Higgs Boson. Beauty in her ability to bear pain and rarely complain as she struggles with her various aches and pains. Beauty in her artistic flair as she splashes her feelings on canvas, abstract to be sure, not my cup of tea, but awesome in the talent it shows. Beauty in her exquisite photographs of sunrises and sunsets that take your breath away.

But then there is the beast that is her. She has a doctorate in procrastination. If something to be done has a deadline, she'll get it done one minute before it is due. Maybe. Her beastly, insidious habit of arguing her point to maddening abstraction, like the time we argued to exhaustion over whether I said we "might" go to the movies that night or we "would." She must always win, no matter how small the point. A beastly anger that reaches frightening proportions. Head banging, fist clenching, screaming, hysterical, sobbing anger. She is an impulse buyer, never coming out of the store with the one item she needed, but several she didn't need. She has no concept of financial management. She can look at her checkbook balance and then go right out and spend twice that amount without a second thought.

In between, she is neither beauty nor beast. Her messiness is, I think, a mark of her ADD. Her dresser is piled high with a variety of makeup bottles, lipsticks, brushes, combs, hair clips, and medicine bottles. Her clothes are half in the closet, half on the floor in front of the closet, and half on her bed. Okay, that's three halves, but it seems like she has that many clothes. In her attempt to organize, she has twenty-four sweater boxes full of odds and ends. She normally keeps these under her bed, but more often they are strewn about the room without tops, the contents in desperate need of sorting. Most of the time, you can't see the floor, and it has been months since I've seen the top of her desk. Her easel and art supplies are in one corner, and I wonder how she can even get to them. Everything in her room is always in disarray, one messy pile moving from one place to another, never disappearing, never getting better.

Two things, though, really define Kristen. First, there's her expansive love. She loves life. She loves everyone. She loves me. Sadly, she is still learning to love herself. Second, and what I love the most about this complex girl, is her courage. I remember all those years ago, when she transitioned in a time when almost no one understood it. Certainly, I didn't, and she had the courage to stand up and tell the world. I feel those tears welling up again and I swallow hard to stem them.

Etched on the back of my eyes is the memory of the night we learned she was transgender. It was a balmy October day, and I paced the kitchen back and forth, peering out of our fourth-floor condominium window that looked out onto a walkway and beyond to the elevator door. I was expecting my son, Christopher, for dinner. I was a nervous wreck as I gazed up and down the walkways for signs of life, hoping to see none. He was already two hours late. Quite frankly, I was hoping the phone would ring and he would cancel altogether.

Once while visiting us, Christopher, then twenty-three, told me that he was a cross dresser, or thought he was one. He said how much he loved to dress in women's clothing and feel the softness of silk on his skin. He said he loved wearing lace and feathers and women's jewelry. While I was stunned and dismayed at the prospect of him living like that, there was little I could do about it. Nor did I try.

Now, four years later in 1995, Christopher asked me if he could come to dinner dressed as a woman. While I dreaded the picture I conjured up in my mind, I agreed. It never occurred to me ask him why, although I wondered why he would want me to see him cross-dressed, but what could I say? I've always felt I should support my children in whatever they did if it wasn't illegal or immoral. I waited with apprehension for the scene Christopher would paint as a woman. Yes, maybe he would cancel.

William, Christopher's stepfather, always the cool head in the family, sat in his favorite chair reading a book, sipping his wine, completely at ease. I kept pacing back and forth along our eternally long entry hall. Fidgety and nervous, I continuously looked in the hall mirror, primping my hair, adjusting my sweater collar, or merely staring at myself for no apparent reason. I kept checking the table settings on the enclosed porch off the living room. I looked out at the neighboring apartment windows filled with lights of evening activity. Although our water view would have added to the ambiance of our dinner, I decided to pull the blinds closed for privacy.

Finally, the doorbell rang and from the porch I shot a panicked look at William as he rose to answer the door. Taking a deep breath, I walked out to greet him, braced myself for what I would find and put on my best "Say cheese" smile. There *she* was. Tall, with beautiful, wavy, shoulder-length blonde hair, and soft brown eyes. Her shapely legs traveled up to a way too short, tight miniskirt, and her otherwise pretty face was obscured by heavy makeup seen only on ladies of the night. That was my introduction to my son, Christopher, the cross dresser. He even called himself "Wendy."

Although I knew he was a cross dresser, seeing him dressed as a female for the first time caught me by surprise. And when I first saw him wearing inappropriate attire, I choked down an "Oh my God." I guess my expectations were that he would at least dress like a refined lady, like myself, not a tramp. He certainly had many women in the family as role models, including his well-dressed sister. In my shock and disappointment, I wanted to spew forth some motherly admonition about appropriate dress, or maybe I really wanted to run away and hide from the reality of this son of mine dressed as woman, or both. It certainly wasn't what I wanted for my son.

To a casual observer, our dinner would have seemed quite normal, even relaxed and enjoyable. Inside, though, my soul was in turmoil as I struggled to appear accepting, amiable, and animated. It felt unnatural to be acting as if nothing was different. My crunched-up shoulders ached, my voice an octave too high, my smile pasted in place. I spilled my glass of wine, kept fiddling with my napkin, wiping my mouth too much, clearing my throat, and spending a socially unacceptable amount of time staring at Wendy.

I sensed that Christopher was also nervous, though he did his best to act as if being Wendy were the most natural thing in the world. He chattered incessantly, waving his hands around as if he were a mime, all of which was unusual for our normally quiet Christopher. He rambled on, telling us of his two-hour plus adventure in dressing and putting on makeup.

"I must have put on my mascara seventeen times."

"It took me over an hour to shave my entire body"

"I couldn't decide what top to wear: the blue, the red, or the green, Mom."

"I took off my lipstick a dozen times trying to find just the right shade."

"I wanted to look perfect for you. Sorry it took me so long to get it together."

He droned on and on and on. I wanted to scream.

STOP. Enough. This is TMI. I really want you to look like a boy, be a boy. I am only tolerating this tonight. Please don't elaborate. Can we talk about something else?

I changed the subject.

"So where are you going tomorrow? A trip to Myakka Park might be nice."

Eventually, I rose to clear the table and Christopher blurted out, "Mom, I'm a girl."

I dropped the fork in my hand and sat down with such force that the chair rocked to one side, almost tossing me on the floor. I was literally speechless. It was one of those moments when your brain is racing to keep up with your heart and nothing comes out of your mouth.

Finally, I said, "What in God's name are you talking about? I've never heard of such a thing. Please explain it to me."

And then, as I remember it, and my memories are fading, I momentarily stopped breathing, waiting for him to answer.

I stared at Christopher for what seemed an eternity. As I think back to that night, I want to rewind the tape and start the evening over as if his statement, "Mom, I'm a girl," never slipped past my handsome son's lips. Since my eldest child was a girl, my dream was always to have a boy as well. One of each as they say. And now this. Another girl? It was unfathomable to me that a boy could be a girl.

How could this brawny male be a girl? How?

With a million questions racing through my mind, tumbling one over the other, I was at last able to regain my composure and, in a tone of utter amazement, ask some questions.

"What do you mean?"

"How do you know?"

"How can this be?"

"Help me out here. This is incredulous."

But, Christopher didn't have all the answers.

Yet.

He just said that he knew he was a girl. He said he was a woman trapped in a male body.

A quiet pall fell over the dinner table and I took that opportunity to clear the table. I retreated to the kitchen, where I could catch my breath as I prepared dessert.

How surreal to be here dishing up something as normal as apple pie and ice cream when Christopher was in the other room claiming to be a girl. I've been through a lot in my life, but this has to be the most bizarre.

As we were eating our dessert, I found myself silently praying the evening would end and I could go back to being just plain me with my son, not this person saying he was a she. I faded in my efforts to be pleasant and pretend that this was just like any other ordinary evening. But the chatter went on as Christopher tried to explain how it was that he felt that he was a girl.

"It's inside of me."

"It's just who I am."

"It's how I want to be."

Then he asked me, "How do you know you're a woman?"

I think of all the questions around the table that evening, that one caught me off guard but helped me understand more than any other what he meant when he said, "I am a girl." I think about that question a lot these days. When I try to answer it, I am at as much of a loss for words to explain it as Christopher was almost twenty years ago. I just know I am a woman. I know, and she knew.

Finally, we ran out of questions and answers, and the uncomfortable silence around the table was our signal that it was time for us to say goodbye. We walked down the walkway to the elevator and I hugged Christopher especially long and tight as we said our goodbyes and I love you's this strange night. I desperately wanted this beautiful boy to know that I loved him and that this turn of events would never change that. I wanted him to know that he would be accepted, always. But loving him and accepting him as a girl still had to be sorted out in my heart. I guess I am still sorting it out, because to this day, I sometimes question if I have accepted his being a girl or am simply resigned to it.

The elevator doors opened, and I watched Christopher walk in and the doors close. Then William and I fell into each other's arms and, in the solitude of the empty walkway with only the stars to watch, I quietly broke down and cried as he comforted me. It no longer mattered to me whether anyone was watching. I had started out years before with a concern Christopher might be gay, then a cross dresser, both of which were mild compared to what I had learned this evening. Where, I wondered, would we go from here? Where would Christopher go from here? Even now, when I least expect it, a tear will silently slip down my cheek for the son I lost and the son I wish I still had but never will again.

EARLY SIGNS

It is the day after our dinner with *Wendy,* and I am lying on my king-size water bed staring up at the ceiling. The sun is streaming in the sliding glass doors leading to the enclosed porch where, just last night, we had that upsetting dinner. I glance around the room to see where William is. As my eyes sweep past the clock, I notice it is way past time to be at work, and I know he is out with the crew. We are property managers for a luxury condominium in Florida, and William manages the outside staff. I'm not going to work today, I think, as I turn over, pull up the covers and clutch my pillow to my chest, as if squeezing it will make it spit out all the answers to all the questions rattling around in my brain.

Did I do something to cause Christopher to be transgender? Why didn't I know? What should I have done differently? Was it because I smoked cigarettes during my pregnancy? Was it because I drank alcohol? Was it because I was on fertility drugs? Was it because I was induced? Why?

Over the years, I continue to search my memory for early

signs Christopher was anything but a male. I think this searching is driven by a nagging nugget in my head that perhaps, in some way, I am responsible for Christopher's gender identity. I have yet to meet a mother who doesn't in one way or another blame herself or take credit for the way her children turn out. This is fueled by the ever-present comments about each child taking after the mother or the father or some relative and, always jokingly, the milkman when two blond, brown-eyed parents produce a blue-eyed, red- headed baby.

What I do remember with crystal clarity is that my sister was born with Down Syndrome. For as long as he lived, my father blamed my mother for her condition. It must have been something she did, or ate, or drank while she was pregnant. It must have been in her family's genetics. We know better today, but we didn't in 1931 when she was born any more than we know today in 2016 what causes gender dysphoria, when a person does not identify with his or her biological physiology.

It has been over twenty years since that morning when my search began, looking for those early indications something wasn't quite right. Often, I come up far short of any overwhelming body of evidence as to the why of his gender identity. Furthermore, any early warning sign would surely have been obscured by Christopher's other tribulations that became manifest as the years went on, most notably narcolepsy, and less understood thirty years ago, attention deficit disorder. Because of his ADD, I often joke that I have the only child on earth who failed kindergarten. It is no longer funny. And with his narcolepsy, I remember rocking him every night for hours on end at 2:00 a.m., trying to get him to sleep. I called him the baby from hell. Together, these conditions created havoc in this gentle person's life, only serving to obfuscate our understanding of his gender persona. Nonetheless, there were distinct indications of his gender dysphoria. If someone had told me to look for them, it might have been acknowledged in time to do something life-changing, or life-saving. But back in the late 1960s and early 1970s, who knew? In fact, science still doesn't know today why a child is born one physical gender but have the other psychological gender. Thankfully, they now recognize those early signs and begin hormone therapy before puberty to prevent changes such as breast development or facial hair.

I roll out of bed and get dressed, hoping maybe I will find some answers lying dormant in the back of my brain. It is 1995 and Google Search doesn't exist. I decide it will be helpful if I start looking for signs as close to conception as I can. After an early miscarriage in 1962, it had taken me six years with the help of brand-new fertility drugs to get pregnant with Christopher. As each month passed and my period arrived, I was becoming more and more discouraged and filled with dread that I might never have another child. One day, after two months, three fertility treatments, and a late period, my gynecologist took a sample of urine to be injected into a rabbit. If the rabbit died, I was pregnant. We didn't have home pregnancy testing kits back then, so finding out if I was pregnant took over a week. The rabbit died, and the doctor estimated I was about six weeks pregnant. I floated out of his office and rushed home to call Tom, Christopher's father, and my then husband, with the news. As I drove home I thought, *only a mother knows this exhilaration when she desperately wants to have a baby and has been trying for years without success.* I turned up the radio and sang along to my favorite Elvis song, "Rock Around the Clock," at the top of my lungs with this silly grin on my face.

The first thing I remember about my pregnancy is I did not have the morning sickness that had accompanied my first gestation. Family and friends kept telling me I was going to have a boy since my experience was totally different from having my daughter. Old wives' tales again. And I remember how huge I got in the first trimester. My doctor suspected I might be having twins or triplets.

What a daunting thought.

I drove home in a daze. When I told Tom, he was not the least bit excited. Two children were enough for him. I thought having twins might be fun since they ran in my family. But to be perfectly honest, the idea of having triplets scared the hell out of me. It didn't make much sense to worry about it, since there was no ultrasound in 1968 and I had to wait until the fifth month for the doctor to hear multiple heartbeats. Thankfully, the doctor only heard one. Phew. I was relieved on the one hand, but disappointed that it wasn't twins on the other. There is simply no pleasing some of us women.

I remember how the baby would kick and move inside of me almost constantly from about the fourth month and with great force. I could often see his hands or feet, or all of them, move from the top of my distended belly to the bottom and back up again, as if he were pushing to get out of the womb or stretching like a newly awakened cat with all four limbs reaching out and stretching at the same time.

Oh joy, oh rapture, five more months of this.

I knew it was going to be a long pregnancy.

In the 1960's knowing the sex of your unborn child was not an option and so, already having a seven-year-old daughter, Tom and I were hoping for a boy. Call it a mother's intuition, but I was so certain the baby would be a boy I didn't even have a name for a girl. The name, Christopher William, had been selected before our first child, Holly, was born. I chose Christopher because I liked it and William after my beloved grandfather Simpson. The Christopher part was more significant to me, since

I erroneously believed it meant, "Gift from God," and to me he was a gift, having taken so much time, energy, and modern science to create. The name means "Christ bearer," so at least it had something to do with the divine.

My labor pains started on a Tuesday and I was certain this would be the day this active baby trying to destroy my uterus would be born. Off to the doctor to check and see. No, not even dilated one millimeter. Perhaps false labor pains. Not ready yet. I was unusually large for having only one baby inside my swollen womb, and I lumbered around the house like a pack mule carrying a year's supply of grub. Sleeping was near impossible from the seventh month on, and my days were spent mostly on the sofa watching TV, tossing and turning trying to find a comfortable position. When these serious pains started, I was hopeful this would be the end of my pregnancy, but they went on and on. No baby for me yet. Was this lengthy labor an early sign of something?

Tom's mother, Adele, was the housekeeper for a family of great wealth and was also a master seamstress for the area rich. Six days later, on the Monday following the beginning of my labor pains, she wanted to give us a tour of the house and grounds of one of her wealthy clients who was out of town. Why not? God knows, I needed a distraction and my labor pains were blessedly minimal. Just after lunch, we arrived at the house and started the tour. My pains started again about midway through the tour and I was holding my stomach and hunching over in pain as each one shot through my body. We finished the grand tour of this opulent house about 4:00 p.m. and were about to walk the vast grounds. I looked out over an expanse the size of at least two football fields and asked her if we were going to walk to the other side of it.

Adele said, “Yes, of course,”

“No, I don’t think so. I need to go home because I’m in labor.”

At 6:00 p.m., we were on our way to the hospital.

Although I had not yet dilated enough for this baby to pop out easily, my doctor decided it was time to induce my labor, or at least more of my labor. I was in such pain and since it had gone on for almost a week, the doctor also wanted to bring this pregnancy to its conclusion. What I didn’t know was that since my abdominal muscle structure was compromised after one pregnancy, I no longer had the strength to push this baby out with normal contractions. My body had been trying for a week, but my muscles were not cooperating. By 7:00 p.m., I had one administration of the labor-inducing drug Pitocin, but it apparently wasn’t enough. At 11:00 p.m., another round was administered. Meanwhile, I was writhing in waves of pain while Tom stood helplessly by my bed holding my hand. His mother sat in the waiting room knitting a blanket for the baby. Was this the cause of Christopher's gender issues? I had recently read there was some speculation that the use of labor-inducing drugs may be linked to autism and brain damage. I did have two doses, so it could be possible. We'll never know.

Hour after hour, I lay in the hospital bed and watched the incessant drip, drip of the IV bag, hoping each drop would be the last and this baby would be born. At 2:00 a.m., the doctor rolled me into the delivery room, hoisted my feet up into the stirrups and commanded me: "Push. Push."

Sweating, groaning, heaving, and yes, yelling expletives at anyone nearby, I kept yelling, "I am! I am!"

But, apparently, I wasn't pushing, as my muscles weren't responding. I desperately wanted my husband to be with me, to hold my hand, to comfort me, but hospital policy forbade it. Maybe it was just as well, as I'm sure I wouldn't have uttered many nice, sweet, or kind words. Finally, at 2:36 a.m. on Tuesday, October 22, 1968, with the aid of mid-forceps, I delivered an eight-pound baby boy already named Christopher William. Were those forceps perhaps an early sign of some neurological issue? Could they have caused a child to be transgender? Sounds silly, but when I was looking for an explanation, all kinds of weird things popped into my head.

As I gazed upon his little face peeking out at me from a

tightly wrapped blue blanket moments after his birth, I was struck by his incredible beauty. Unlike our daughter, who was the normal wrinkled, red, and at first glance, rather unattractive baby, Christopher was perfect in his lack of those newborn features. He was so beautiful I thought he should have been a girl. Physically, Christopher was male from head to toe. No doubt about it. But, such a pretty boy. I believe this was another early sign this baby was different.

Holding him in my hospital room later that morning I felt awkward. I didn't know how to talk to him, as if I instinctively knew something was just not right. At first, I found myself talking to him as if he were our Scottish terrier, Angus, talking to him with a mixture of baby talk and mother-babble, not distinctly one or the other. When that didn't work, I just kept looking at his perfect face, hoping the right words would come. Of course, they eventually did, but my early uneasiness still bothers me from time to time.

I really wanted to say things like, "Oh, what a pretty little baby girl you are!"

But, that wasn't right. I still feel a mother, of all people, should know how to interact with her child, whatever the gender, and I didn't seem to be able to. It wasn't easy for me. In fact, at first, it was almost impossible. So, I just sat there and rocked him, waiting for the nurse to come and retrieve him.

Why did I feel as if Christopher was some strange alien with whom I had trouble connecting? Was it a mother's sixth sense that something was not right, or some psychic knowing that this child was not a boy? Who can say? It still troubles me, though, because I feel that I should have plumbed the depths of my feelings a bit more, wondered why more, found an answer if one was to be had. Being young, foolish, and somewhat insecure, I didn't. To this day, however, and I don't know why, my first uncomfortable encounter with Christopher pops into my consciousness and is etched on my heart.

In 1968, just after the birth of Christopher, the estate that owned our rented 1734 farmhouse was put up for sale, including our home. Unfortunately, at just about the same time Tom was laid off from his job. As a consequence of these events, we found ourselves looking for housing in another state, where Tom eventually found a job. Thus, when Christopher was but eight months old, we moved from our old familiar farmhouse we had lived in for over eight years into a newly built, three-bedroom raised-ranch in New England. It was for us a dream house, brand new, with all the room one would ever need with two children. It sat on a half-acre, so there was plenty of room to plant my garden, set up the children's swing set, stretch out, and live. It had a deck, a patio, and a large family room downstairs with a cozy fireplace. It was littered with pink girly toys like Barbie and gender-neutral Fisher Price toys for boys under the age of one.

Our new neighborhood, unlike our old one, was populated with young couples with children of all ages and genders. This turned out to be a godsend for both Holly and Christopher, as many of the families had four, five, or even six children, giving both kids many opportunities to make friends. I always encouraged my children to have their friends visit and play at our home. Neighborhood kids congregated at our place because we lived at the base of a small hill, and the street in front of our house was a level cross street between two hilly roads and perfect for playing games.

On any given day, there were girls playing jump rope or hopscotch, while the boys played kickball and football. Our expansive front yard was the scene of many neighborhood baseball games, and the woods and creek in the back of our house were perfect for little boys to find frogs and insects and play hide and seek. The large family room was a great space to set up a big table and invite in the neighborhood children to do a variety of arts and crafts. Once, we made little sailing ships out of walnut shells and sailed them in the bathtub. On another occasion, we took to the kitchen for a taffy pull, with strings of taffy everywhere, icky sticky hands flying up in the air, and laughter bouncing off the walls. We laughed until our sides hurt.

From the living room window, I would watch Christopher

join in playing with the neighborhood boys, riding his bike around the neighborhood and batting a ball. Usually, however, I saw him playing with a neighbor girl, Laura, who lived just across the street from us and was his same age. I recall thinking how odd for him to be spending so much time with a girl beginning at age three, but I also thought, “So what?”

I’d ask him when he came home, “Hi Tiger,” His father’s nickname for him. “What were you and Laura doing?” He would tell me he was playing house with her, or hide and seek, or they were pretending to bake cookies. Nothing harmful. I might have been upset if he had told me he was playing doctor and nurse, but he never did. No one else said anything about the amount of time he spent with Laura, so there were no red flags about sexual orientation/identification, nor was it something even on my radar screen. It’s another sign I missed. And, I must say, “Wow, a real, in-your-face, early sign.”

As a toddler and young boy, Christopher had a thick head of beautiful blond hair. And, like many young couples with a stay-at-home mom, we lived on a shoestring, so it was up to me to cut his hair. He loved to keep his hair long and would put up such a fuss when I wanted to cut it short. I would almost always let him have his way. He wore it in a shoulder length Dutch boy style and looked like a girl except for the fact that he wore overalls or pants with plain cotton tops. On dress-up days, he wore his littleman suit and a clip-on bow tie. But it was the late1960s and early 1970s, so who cares about the length of one's hair? Many men were wearing shoulder length hair, so I didn't give it a second thought. Again, though, another early sign?

I remember so well the trips I made to the bank to deposit our checks with a four-year-old Christopher in tow. I always used the drive-up window because it was quicker. With his long hair and beautiful face, the teller always asked, "Would your little girl like a lollipop?"

"Oh yes, thank you. But he's a boy."

"I'm sorry. He's just such a pretty child, I thought...."

Since this had been a regular occurrence for many years from many different tellers, I continued to tell all of them Christopher was a boy and would just love a lollipop. One day as we were driving away, I asked, "Does it bother you people think you are a girl?"

"No, it doesn't."

I thought that a bit odd, but I still didn't tumble to anything out of the ordinary. It did, however, annoy me when people thought he was a girl, particularly one who was four years old and should look like his gender. I vowed to cut his hair shorter for the next trip to the bank.

There were other signs all was not "normal." Once, my jewelry disappeared from my jewelry box and I was frantic. I thought one of the neighborhood children who wandered in and out of the house on a regular basis had stolen it. There wasn't anything of much value in the small cookie tin I called a "jewelry" box, but it was all I had and now it was gone. No more earrings or bracelets to wear, no more pretty necklaces to match with my various outfits. Fortunately, I wore my wedding and engagement ring, which were the only pieces of any worth. Day after day, I searched high and low for my jewelry until I knew the contents of every drawer, closet, niche, and nook in the house by heart. I asked my friends, my children, my spouse, anyone if they had seen it. Nothing. After about three weeks I finally gave up and began rebuilding my collection a pair of earrings at a time. It was six weeks later when Christopher "found" my jewelry, or so he said, in the hall linen closet. The hall linen closet is right next to the master bedroom door and right across the hall from Christopher's room, a convenient place to dump something. Of course, I had already investigated the linen closet repeatedly when the jewelry first went missing and found nothing. So, when he "found" it there, I knew something was strange. And although these odd feelings of strangeness signaled something weird going on, the last thing I would connect it to in terms of Christopher would be his sexual orientation.

And then there was the time he was six when I found him sitting in the middle of his room trying on a pair of white, girl's tights. They belonged to his cousin, Kim, who was sleeping in the second twin bed in his room while her family visited.

I said, “What are you doing?”

After a bit of squirming and looking down at the floor, he answered, “I’ll tell you when I’m nine!” How odd, I thought, but brushed it aside as child’s play.

In his six-year-old mind, nine was a time far, far in the future. What now amazes me about the incident is that even at such an early age he knew. He knew. I didn’t. I didn’t have a clue.

As Christopher grew older, there were other times when I would find him with female clothing. Once, I discovered him sleeping in a pair of my pantyhose. Another time, I discovered my evening gowns in his closet. He mumbled excuse upon excuse. For example, he once said his high school girlfriend wanted to try on my dresses. I didn’t buy his excuse. First, I was a size eight and she was a size sixteen. None of my clothes or Christopher’s sister’s clothes would fit her.

With the panty-hose episode, he said they kept his legs warm at night. Again, I was skeptical, because there were many other ways to keep warm at night, like socks or another blanket. The excuses were so contrived that over time, they only led me to believe perhaps Christopher was gay or a cross dresser.

I knew he was hiding something. I was always puzzled by

this behavior, but never afraid of it. I just could never quite figure out why he was fooling around with all these female items. I guess if being transgender were as well-publicized as it is today, I could have put two and two together and come up with my future daughter.

I suppose if I had been prejudiced against gays or cross dressers, I might have been more upset thinking he might be one of them. But gays, lesbians, cross-dressers and the like were simply a part of my everyday landscape in the community theater milieu of my high school and early wedded life. That there might be serious social consequences for a homosexual or cross dressing child never crossed my mind because I never experienced it with any of my LGBT friends.

I guess you might say I was rather naïve. Had I known of any such discrimination, I might have felt more negatively toward having a homosexual son, since I would have understood it would mean a more difficult life for him. But I do know that no matter what, I would have still loved him, because he would always be my son. I also know we all have this deep desire to have children who are what society would consider “normal.” A girly girl, a rough and tumble boy. What is that poem: “What are Little Girls Made Of? Sugar and spice and everything nice. What are Little Boys Made Of? Snips and snails and puppy dogs’ tails.” And, my Christopher wasn’t either it seemed.

In 1983, we moved from our raised ranch to a three-story townhouse on Long Island Sound. I recall so vividly one day when Christopher, then sixteen, sat on the bottom steps going up to the third-floor loft. I came up carrying a load of laundry and saw him just sitting there with a rather pensive look on his face. I put the laundry down on the landing, sat next to him, and said, "What's up?"

"Not much, mom. I have a test tomorrow."

"Oh. Well, I hope you do well on it. Have you studied?"

"Yeah, a little. I don't really like history."

"I didn't either when I was your age, but I do now."

"When are we going to eat?"

"I'm going to start dinner as soon as I put the laundry away. Anything special you want?"

"No, not really. Mom, I have a secret I can't tell anyone."

"You can tell me. I'm your mom and you can tell me anything. I promise I won't get mad or judge you."

"I know, Mom, but I'm just not ready to tell you."

My first thought was that he was going to verify my suspicions of his homosexuality. Although he wasn't ready to tell me this great secret, I felt compelled to ask him if he were gay.

"Are you gay?"

He responded in one of those teen-aged tones.

"Moooommm, no, I'm not gay."

"Did you get your girlfriend pregnant?"

"No, Mom, I didn't."

"Are you in trouble with the law? Did you get a speeding ticket? Were you doing drugs?"

"Noooooooo. Nooooooo. Mom, stop asking me. I just can't tell you right now, but someday I will."

Well, I thought, I can cross all those off my list, but then I was even more puzzled as to what his secret might be. At least I understood homosexuality, unwanted pregnancy, pot, tickets, a run-in with the law. And if it wasn't any of those, what could it be? What I did know was Christopher wasn't telling. We ended the conversation rather awkwardly, and I left to put the laundry away, wondering if Christopher would ever tell me his secret.

As Christopher developed out of puberty and into a young man, his slim 5'9" physique was definitely masculine, with broad shoulders, slim hips, moderate body hair, and facial hair now needing to be shaved. From a physical perspective, there was no reason to suspect anything to do with his gender. And obviously, I hadn't caught on to any of the early signs in front of me from the time Christopher was born. It might be different today, since we know so much more about these transgender children. Had I known more or recognized the early signs, my child would not have had to suffer through such a torment of understanding, explaining, and accepting his female gender.

AND ON TOP OF ALL THAT

Christopher's gender issues often took a back seat to a myriad of other stressful situations in our family. Most involved him, but others involved myself, my marriage, and circumstances that impacted our lives together. It would take another book to go into a lot of detail. But in this chapter, I will try to give you a flavor of the total fabric of the family life in which Christopher lived. Life is messy. We don't live in a vacuum, and our sexuality or gender issues are a part of life, not the whole of life.

Christopher was lactose intolerant from birth and the four-month struggle to figure out his disorder was exhausting. Every time I would feed him, he would throw up. I could handle that. What was more stressful was that the vomiting was also accompanied by severe diarrhea. I kept the company that makes A & D Ointment in business just trying to keep Christopher's little fanny free from a nasty, raw rash.

There were no disposable diapers at the time, so our diaper service bill was outrageous. Furthermore, as he grew older, if he just happened to have even a small amount of milk in anything he ate, he would have to go on a regimen of bananas mixed with his soy milk, Prosobee, until his symptoms abated, which could take several weeks. I dreaded facing every day with this baby. I was exhausted most of the time and fearful of taking him out in case he had an accident. Fortunately, I was a stay-at-home mom until he was almost four. But day after day of stuff coming out of both ends wore me down.

In 1970, while visiting my mother in California, she gave Christopher some ice cream and we were off and running on the banana route. One night at the dinner table he reached up and over the tray of his high chair to grab a piece of chicken off the dish as it was being passed. He was hungry and ready for some solid food. My heart broke as I took it away from him, but the consequences would have been quite unpleasant for both of us. On balance, however, we kept his episodes under control by carefully watching what he ate.

Christopher was five when he outgrew his lactose intolerance. Until then, we had to try him on some dairy product every three months to see if he was still intolerant, which usually resulted in at least two to three weeks of uncontrollable diarrhea and the banana diet. You can imagine how he rebelled against that diet after a few days. Even I rebelled against those times of testing his condition, as it also meant I had to steel myself for the onslaught of consequences. It was a constant battle and I was filled with guilt about feeding my child a less than nourishing meal day after day, all the while silently hoping this time would be the last.

After having a near perfectly behaved first child who ate and slept on schedule and was what I had expected of a child, this second one was off the charts. I was totally unprepared physically and emotionally for this child, but somehow, I found the inner strength to face each day with the hidden hope that maybe next day or next month, everything would change and all would be normal. Coping with his lactose intolerance was one thing, but because of his narcolepsy, Christopher's lack of a sleeping routine was even more stressful. He would sleep for a few hours and be up for many, or he would sleep for many and be up for a few. I would be a wealthy woman if I had a nickel for every minute I spent in a rocking chair trying to lull him to sleep. When I found myself falling asleep with him nestled in the crook of my neck, I would put him in his crib and leave him to fall asleep on his own. But he would cry a long soulful wail, pulling at my heart. So, of course, I would drag myself out of bed and into the rocking chair with this wide-awake little boy. Would this never end?

He climbed out of his crib at ten months old, so we installed extension sides. He also started walking and was covered with bruises from falling. Since it appeared I might be abusing him, I was embarrassed to take him to the doctor for his check-up.

Gratefully, the doctor understood, but Christopher's early mobility only added to our problems. At twelve months, he was up and over the extension rails on his crib and out of the net we had covering the top. By the time he was fifteen months old, we had stored the crib in the attic and bought him a single bed. He seemed so tiny in that bed that I feared that he would fall out every night. He never did.

Hearing a clatter one night at 4:00 a.m. I got up and found my two-year old Christopher in the kitchen mixing up a batch of just about anything he could get his hands on and one burner on the stove searing hot. When I asked him what he was doing he said, "I'm making cookies."

Bless his little heart. He had no idea he was doing anything out of the ordinary.

"Well, it's still nighttime, so let's go to bed and we can make cookies when it is daytime."

I hustled him off to bed and lay awake the rest of the night, worrying that he would be up and cooking something on the stove again.

His nocturnal wanderings had begun. Short of staying up all night to watch him, I had no idea what to do about it. I was at my sleepless wit's end. After unrelenting anxious nights listening for Christopher, I mentioned the problem to his pediatrician, who suggested we put a chain on his bedroom door to contain him at night if he got up to wander. This, he said, would keep Christopher in, but allow him to see out and not feel locked up. I was horrified at the suggestion. While I doubted the wisdom of it, I had no better answer. I felt terrible locking my beloved toddler in his room. I went to bed every night feeling guilty. By this time guilt was my constant companion, because I felt as if I was abusing or abandoning my baby. I can't remember when we took the chain off his bedroom door, but I knew that he was old enough to understand that wandering around the house was forbidden. He still woke up at all hours, but eventually he knew enough to stay in his own room, and I could get more than a couple of hours of sleep myself.

At about age five, it became more and more evident there was more to Christopher's behavioral problems than dairy and sleep. He didn't respond to normal developmental stimuli for a child his age. For example, he never responded to either reward or punishment in order to learn a behavior. He never learned how to clean his room, and whether I threw all of his toys away or left them in a mess on his bedroom floor, there was no change in his attitude or behavior. What, I would ask myself, did I have to do to help him fit in, be normal? Be like his sister. Be like all the neighborhood kids. I'd even settle for a clean room.

As I mentioned earlier, Christopher had trouble with school in kindergarten and this continued all through his school years.

He was a constant underachiever at school. He didn't pay attention in class, ignored assignments, and rarely completed a task. When he liked a subject, as he did his photography class, he dove right in and did beautifully. Otherwise, forget it. Staying after school didn't bother him. He didn't care whether he went to school or not, whether his teacher and parents praised him or chided him, whether he passed or failed. Telephone calls came from his teacher weekly and were always frustrating. No matter what we tried, whether it was cookies or criticism, Christopher seemed oblivious and nothing made any change in his behavior. While it may not have bothered him, it certainly bothered me. I dreaded every phone call during school hours. No one seemed to have any way to motivate him.

When he was seven years old, I was discouraged with my pediatrician and his lack of ability in helping me cope with Christopher. I made the decision to take him to our family doctor and see if he could help. I knew this kid had problems, but no one knew just what was causing them. I needed some help and some answers. After I recited the litany of Christopher's life to our family doctor, he suggested we try a new drug, Ritalin, for a couple of weeks and see what happened.

It was the best two weeks in both my life and in Christopher's life. I was ecstatic over this amazing change in his behavior. He seemed to calm down and focus on his tasks in school.

For the first time in seven years, he was able to get about six hours of sleep at night and wake up refreshed in the morning. But my euphoria was short-lived. After two weeks on the drug, his father refused to have his son raised on drugs and I was not allowed to continue the treatment. I was frustrated and disappointed and simply couldn't understand Tom's reticence about continuing a drug that was obviously so helpful. How sad that was for all of us, but at the time it didn't occur to me to demand a different outcome or fight harder to continue this wonderful treatment. I was raised to defer to my husband, so I did. This was in 1975 and ADD and ADHD had not even begun to poke their heads out of the clouds into the reality of people's life. So, we didn't really have a definitive diagnosis.

The struggle continued. What had been weekly phone calls from school were now every other day. Mostly, the calls were about how Christopher wasn't motivated, wasn't listening, didn't do his homework, didn't pay attention, didn't participate. Didn't. Didn't. Didn't. Always the same – he was failing everything. Most parents have yearly parent/teacher conferences. Ours were quarterly. It was exhausting and frustrating. Nothing seemed to be working, nothing was changing. I felt so helpless and unable to make a difference in my son's life.

A typical day with Christopher would begin with the onerous chore of trying to get him to wake up. He had always had an erratic pattern of sleeping, or not. Although he was often awake in the wee hours of the morning, he was usually in a deep sleep at 7:00 a.m. Being half asleep most of the time meant I had to get his clothes out, goad him incessantly to get dressed, and get him to the breakfast table. Many mornings, he walked to the bus stop a block away eating a pop-tart because his dawdling made him late.

After school, Christopher would stay with a neighbor until I picked him up in the late afternoon, since I was either in school, or later, holding down a full-time job. Then the homework struggle would begin. Often, he would tell me that he didn't have any homework or that he had done it in school. I would then learn later when his teacher called that he hadn't done his homework. Christopher was more interested in riding his bicycle through the neighborhood than paying attention to schoolwork. And while many children feel this way, I like to think that most also have a sense of responsibility that at some point homework needs to get done. Christopher didn't have this, at least not as far as I could tell.

We always had dinner at 5:30 p.m. when Tom was working days or at 3:30 p.m. when he worked second shift. Dinner in our house was never one of those times when we all sat around and casually talked about our day or shared jokes and stories. It was more like a ten-minute break in the day. I was often annoyed that

I had taken hours to prepare a nice meal and it was gone in ten minutes. No one seemed particularly relaxed. On occasion, Tom's verbal criticism would send one, or all of us, away from the table angry or in tears.

After dinner, if the homework hadn't been finished, Christopher and I would sit at the kitchen table and agonizingly work on whatever it was that needed doing. I was never good at math. While I tried hard, I was never able to help Christopher with the "new" math. Science projects were a virtual horror, because I never knew about them until the last minute. Then all hell broke loose as we scrambled to get it done on time. I remember one day when we had to make a topographical papier mache map of the United States on a two by three-foot piece of plywood that was due the next day. It was 1:00 a.m. by the time we finished, and I was not a happy camper. I must say, though, that I did learn where all fifty states were located. One would have thought I would have communicated with the teachers and asked them to mail me homework assignments, but I didn't. Damn. It might have made my life a bit easier. I now understand what "Old too soon, smart too late," means.

Evenings after homework, were generally quiet as the children watched TV, read, or played. Bedtime was another eternal struggle. Christopher often wasn't tired and didn't want to go to bed. Bedtime was usually 8:30 p.m. or maybe even 9:00 p.m.

First, I had to convince him to get into his pajamas. Then I had to coax him to get into bed. By that time, I would be tired, cranky, and pissed off, because it wasn't going smoothly, and Tom wasn't helping. He considered bedtime duties women's work. Finally, teeth brushed, bathed, and in bed, it was time to read the "bedtime story."

I always had this idea that if I didn't read to my kids I was a bad mother. My mother never read to me, so I didn't have a role model. Somewhere along the line, I decided it was something I should do. Christopher's favorite story was *Little Bear*. I read it so often I almost had it memorized. Quite frankly, I groaned after a while when he insisted on having it read to him. When the story was finished and it was time to turn off the lights and close the door, Christopher often mentioned that he saw monsters and animals in his room, so I would leave his closet light on and his door cracked open a bit.

The nights were rough. Often, Christopher would come across the hall and get into bed with us. Another struggle – the "you have to be a big boy and sleep in your own bed," struggle. It was a good thing we had a king size bed, for many times he was with us until morning. Again and again, he would tell us he was seeing those monsters or animals trying to get him. I chalked that up to childhood imagination. If I was still awake when he had finally fallen asleep, I would pick him up and put him in his own bed. He kept this routine up until he was ten, when suddenly it stopped without any rhyme or reason. Odd, I thought, but I was more relieved than curious enough to figure out why. Sometimes, just the fatigue of dealing with him on a day-to-day basis made it easier for me to simply accept the situation and stop searching for answers.

And so our mornings, our evenings, and our nights with Christopher were often strung out like a taffy pull, and we were the sagging part in the middle. What, I often wondered, were we going to do to help this troubled child? You see, I knew he was not normal and something was causing his unusual behavior. But what?

When Christopher was in sixth grade, we had a battery of Learning Disability tests done, as well as intelligence tests. He tested in the ninety-ninth percentile of intelligence with no learning disabilities. More frustration. We even had Christopher meet with an educational counselor for two years. Nothing helped. Nothing changed. Some days I felt as if I were in this huge maze and no matter which way I turned, there was simply no way out and nowhere to turn.

The constant confrontations in my life always put me in a bad mood, often angry and confused.

Why me? Why does this child have to make my life so miserable?

Furthermore, Tom was little help. He worked all day, worked on his cars after dinner, and then went to bed. He was as confused as I was about how best to deal with Christopher, and he dealt by avoiding it. The stress and sole responsibility of this wore me down, but I somehow still managed to keep putting one foot in front of the other as my life was slowly unraveling.

Somewhere in this muddle of life, if you take time to notice, there is always a sliver of sunshine. Mine, as chief cook, was that Christopher was at least a good eater. He wasn't a fussy eater, except for tomatoes, which he refused to eat. I also had to spoon feed him broccoli and tell him it was "trees." To this day, we laughingly refer to them as trees. In general, amid all his problems, Christopher was a pleasant, laughing child with a positive attitude who was always willing to share.

I remember once in the grocery store, I bought him a package of chewing gum. As we were checking out, he was happily giving all the kids around a piece of his gum. God bless him. Sunshine always brings a smile to my face, particularly when it involves either of my children. Despite having a problem child, he was mine. I loved him with all my heart, warts and all. I always try to find some sunshine in my life so the darkness isn't overwhelming.

At the end of eighth grade, the headmaster at his private day school suggested that a boarding school that helped "difficult" children might help Christopher. We would have preferred a local day school where we could have Christopher at home with us, but none would accept him due to his poor academic record. So, off he went at the beginning of ninth grade to a private boarding school in New York that was known to take underachieving children.

I had mixed feelings about this decision from the beginning. On one hand, I felt that I was failing my child, that I couldn't raise him, that I wasn't a good mother, and had to send my child away. On the other hand, I think I was somewhat relieved. It meant I wouldn't have to deal with the daily struggle, the school failures, the fitful sleep patterns, all of it. But I felt guilty... again. Guilt was becoming my second name. To this day, I carry this sense of guilt about those years we sent him away. Plus, I wasn't a good communicator when he was gone. I remember him once asking me to write him a letter once a week so that he would get some mail. How sad I felt when he made that request. From then on, I tried to pay him more attention. I'm not sure I succeeded.

In retrospect, sending Christopher to boarding school was a big mistake. It gave Christopher an unsupervised sort of freedom that he was simply not capable of handling. While he managed to squeak by with minimal grades, he also began to use drugs. In 1985, he was expelled one month before the end of his junior year of high school for bringing marijuana onto the campus. While I was deeply disappointed in his behavior, the other part of me was relieved that he was coming home.

Intermingled in our cloud of life and coping with the travails of Christopher's life over the years, I had other stressful situations to deal with in my marriage to Tom. From the time Christopher was three, I had been a full-time student at Sacred Heart University and worked two part-time jobs to pay for my tuition and child care. I was not home a great deal of the time, although I was usually home in the afternoon when Holly and Christopher came home from school. After graduating with a degree in Chemistry in 1975, I went to work full-time for the first time since my marriage sixteen years earlier.

I could see this constant concern for Christopher, my absence daily, and a husband who wasn't much help and who, for two years, worked the second shift, were taking a toll on our marriage. We often didn't see much of each other even when we were both at home. We both began to drink heavily and argue frequently. Tom would withdraw to his garage and work on his cars while I was left with all the normal duties of taking care of a husband, two children, and a household, all the while either keeping up with a full academic schedule, the homework school entailed, or a long commute and workday. Quite literally, I was exhausted, strung out, and near the breaking point.

To cap it all off, one day, Tom quit his job without consulting me, bought a parcel of land with funds borrowed from my mother, and built a house in a town some forty minutes away. He was supposed to sell it and move on to build another house and become a house builder. He didn't. He wanted me to move into the house. I refused. It would mean almost an hour commute to my job. We argued about this constantly. But there was more, much more.

I think I might have tolerated the arguing and alienation, but seventeen years into our marriage, Tom, along with the drinking, had become physically abusive. I never knew what would set him off or when he would erupt. The first time he attacked me was on our powerboat in the summer of 1976 as we were anchored in the middle of Long Island Sound. Tom and Christopher were up on the bow of the boat pulling up the anchor. Up with the anchor came a tiny little crab. Christopher, being a curious little child of seven, wanted to keep it. Tom told him he had to throw it back and Christopher started crying. When I poked my head around the corner and asked Tom what was wrong, he ran back to me, threw me inside the cabin, and began banging my head against the walls as he choked me. Our neighbor was with us with two of her children. After she locked the younger one in the forward cabin with Christopher, she somehow managed to get Tom to stop beating on me. I thought he was going to kill me. On the way back to port, I sat on the bow of the boat alone, drenched in fear, determined this would not go on. I would no longer defer to my husband. If I valued myself and my life, this life had to stop. I would get a divorce, I thought. Little did I know then it would continue for another two years, because I didn't really know how to wrench myself out of such an untenable situation.

For me, the breaking point came in 1978 as I was driving to the airport in Erie, Pennsylvania, to catch a plane home from my consulting assignment. A year earlier, I had taken a job with a Fortune 500 company as an internal consultant in their Manufacturing Logistics Department. The upside was that it paid a lot more money, but the downside was that it required I travel out of state about 50 percent of the time. No one really liked my travel schedule, especially Tom. I am certain my children didn't either. At that point, we were all under more stress than one should reasonably have to endure. As I approached the airport entrance, I pulled the car over to the side of the road and broke down sobbing. I cried long and hard and barely made my plane, but I knew the time had come to end my marriage. I called a lawyer the next day.

I never realized how emotionally difficult it would be to end a nearly twenty-year marriage, even though I desperately wanted it over. I cried so many tears for so many days I thought I might die from dehydration. After four months of agonizingly working out the details, we were granted a divorce. I remember the catch in my throat when the judge asked if I wanted to go back to using my maiden name. I paused for what seemed like forever, holding back tears because it represented the finality of this act. When the judge asked me a second time, I whispered "No."

I kept Tom's name because it was my name professionally, and it was my children's last name. It was the only vestige of my marriage that I kept. My divorce was certainly not a happy event for anyone, but I know it saved my sanity.

Of course, the divorce didn't solve Christopher's problems, nor did it alleviate them. Before I married my second husband, William, I told him that Christopher was not your normal eleven-year-old. I have to admit that I was racked with uncertainty about how best to tell William about Christopher. I didn't want to lose his love due to all of Christopher's issues, but I knew that was a possibility. Not telling him was just not an option. So, with my heart in my throat, clammy hands, and a lot of apprehension, we had several long talks about my son. I didn't leave out any of the details.

William, I have learned, is a caregiver. He loves to take care of people. I believe that it was this trait in him that caused him to see Christopher as someone he could take care of and fix. He wasn't turned off by all of Christopher's issues but rather seemed to think he could truly make a difference in this child's life. He had three children, one a son, and he was convinced that by involving Christopher in Little League, skiing, Indian Guides, and the like, by giving of his time to be with him, he could transform Christopher into a normal boy without issues. In William's mind. these activities were all things boys liked to do and Tom had not done with Christopher. With my history with Christopher, I wasn't sure William's efforts would make a bit of difference. I prayed they would, and I was relieved he hadn't left running.

Well, William was wrong. Yes, Christopher enjoyed things like skiing, but he hated tennis and Little League baseball. And there were fun things they did together, like taking in a baseball game, visiting a museum, or playing a game of catch. But none of these father-son bonding activities made any difference in Christopher's behavior. William couldn't fix Christopher any more than I could. Neither could the doctors, counselors, or private schools. Christopher was an unfathomable challenge. With nowhere else to turn, I decided I had to see if Christopher had a physical problem.

At age fifteen, in the summer of 1984, Christopher was officially diagnosed with narcolepsy by an endocrinologist and put on Dexedrine. We have learned part of the disease is hypnogogic hallucinations, which accounted for all those monsters and animals he was seeing in his room at night. He had them almost nightly. Occasionally they frightened him so much that he asked me to stay with him until he fell asleep. I would lie down next to him in his bed and cradle his head in my arms until he fell asleep, all the time desperately wanting to make him whole. The diagnosis as a narcoleptic helped explain some of his behavior problems, but certainly not all of them. Fortunately, with the Dexedrine, he was at least able to wake up in a little under an hour and go to school fully awake. But his problems were far, far from over and beyond our understanding of them. They were still so vague.

Years later, as an adult, Christopher was officially diagnosed with ADD and with the type of ADD that affects executive function. The debilitating feature of this type of ADD is the person's total inability to plan and execute a task, and it helped explain some things for me. Going from A to B was impossible for these people. I remember once Christopher told me that while he knew what he wanted to do in his head, he couldn't find a way to make it happen. Since he couldn't predict that anything he did would come out perfectly, he simply wouldn't try. Sadly, we couldn't recognize the implications of this disability to get from A to B until decades later. When Christopher repeatedly told me that he couldn't clean his room, he literally meant he couldn't clean his room. Furthermore, there really is no cure for this condition. They don't even know what causes it, except to say that the brain is not wired correctly, or even scarier, not connected at all in certain areas. I wonder if they will ever sort out the mystery of the brain and can help people with things like narcolepsy and ADD.

Life presented me with just too many layers of complexity to keep Christopher's sexuality at the top of my list of daily concerns. But then, no one's life is monochromatic, and I find that living with Christopher is much more colorful than I ever imagined. I mean really, how many mothers can say, "My son is my daughter, but that's not what screws him up," with a straight face?

GOOD LORD, DELIVER US

In 1983, on an impulse at the NY Boat Show, we traded in our thirty-foot Catalina sailboat and bought a new, thirty-six-foot Catalina. Life seemed idyllic. Christopher was in boarding school, so I didn't have to face the day-to-day struggles of dealing with his problems. Together, William and I were earning a respectable income and enjoying the fruits of our labors. We were practicing Christians and had a circle of friends from church, work, and our boating community. Yes, life was good. Too good.

From the spring of 1985, when Christopher came home after being expelled from school to the fall of 1986, I juggled my job and travel demands, as well as acting as a referee between William and Christopher, who had developed an intense adversarial relationship toward each other. William was angry and frustrated at what Christopher was doing to our lives. Christopher was afraid of William. William didn't trust Christopher, and Christopher didn't trust William. What would start as a difference of opinion between them would escalate into screaming bouts and then on to physical attacks.

Often, if I was disagreeing with Christopher, William would feel obligated to defend me and go after him. More often than I want to think about or acknowledge, these two men (for Christopher was now fully grown physically) would literally get into a shoving, screaming match, each one challenging the other to "hit me," or goading the other to take some action. Caught in the middle, being torn like a rope in a tug-of-war, I would become frightened to the point of sheer terror and start my own screaming and yelling match, begging them to stop. It was only when I would finally throw my body in between them that they would stop. They would go off to their corners like boxers separated during a bout to catch their breath, but I would be drained emotionally and physically and not sure if we could continue to live together. The house was always awkwardly silent after these encounters.

I am now certain these encounters were even worse when I was out of town and couldn't intervene, but that was also the only time I had any solitude in which to re-energize my failing spirit. Although it didn't help me cope at the time, something I now realize is that William was a stepparent trying to be a parent. Stepparents must earn a stepchild's respect before they can even begin to be a disciplinarian or even, at times, offer advice. A stepparent must first work on establishing a solid, positive, relationship with the child. With Christopher, this was difficult to the point of being impossible. Their adversarial relationship was fueled by this lack of respect on either side. Looking back, it should come as no surprise that I did not cope well with the continual stress.

Late in 1986, it all came to a head when I became suicidal and ended up spending a year in serious counseling. I often felt like the victim in a Victorian drama when, in fact, it was the two of them who were going at each other. I often wondered why I was the one in counseling. The pain of being torn to shreds between the two men I loved most in the world was gnawing away at me until, with no place to turn for respite, I simply gave up.

I was told that I tried to commit suicide three times, but I remember only one time when the pain and distress from being torn between William and Christopher caused me to want to die. It's not something I talk about, but then I would imagine anyone who tries to kill themselves never does talk much about it. One evening, after another one of William and Christopher's fighting matches, I left them making up with each other. Almost in a daze, I headed for our bedroom on the second floor. I walked in, closed the door, and looked around for some way to take my life.

The pain, actual physical pain, was unbearable. We didn't have a gun or a bottle of sleeping pills. Our master suite had an en suite bathroom, and I wandered in and looked around. I'm not sure what I was looking for at that exact moment. I looked up and saw the shower head.

Good. You can hang yourself.

I went into my closet and removed the sash from my bathrobe. I climbed up onto the edge of the tub and looped the sash around the shower head. I pulled on it to see if it would hold my weight. I thought it would, because I only weighed about 110 pounds. Then I climbed over the edge of the tub, put my head through the loop I had made, and let my legs fall into the tub. The sash held. I started to get dizzy and lightheaded. It was peaceful. I had no more pain. Then the sash slipped off the shower head and I fell into the tub, dazed.

After hearing me fall, William ran into the bathroom, scooped me up in his arms, and carried me to our bed. The details of what happened next are fuzzy, but I never tried to kill myself again. We started family counseling the next week. I know that the experience made me realize I was at the lowest point in my entire life, and something had to change. God only knows what it did to the hearts and souls of William and Christopher, but we all needed healing.

It was during this time of upheaval that Christopher told me he had a secret he couldn't tell anyone. Of course, I was convinced he was gay. So, being a vigilant mother, I began to look for the signs. None came. In fact, in his senior year of high school, Christopher found a girlfriend and often brought her home after school. Her name was Mariah. At our first meeting, I knew she was definitely not the type of girl that I wanted for my son. First, she was overweight, and I was a fanatic about keeping my weight in line. This was a throwback to my first husband, who would tell me I was chubby if I was even five pounds heavier than he thought I should be. Second, she wore way too much makeup. Third, she wore clothing that suggested that she wanted sex…now. Fourth, she couldn't keep her hands to herself. Fifth, I didn't think she was very bright. Aha, I thought, Christopher is in lust, something every mother should realize about a sixteen-year-old boy. His relationship with her did, for the time being, alleviate my anxiety over the issue of his gayness.

Adding still more fuel to the fire, my hopes Christopher would graduate from high school were dashed when, two weeks before graduation, we were told he was failing every class, would not graduate, and had to repeat the twelfth grade. He dropped out. Type A mother that I am, I immediately signed him up to take the GED exams the following month. I piled him kicking and screaming into the car and dropped him off at the test center. Eight hours later, I picked him up. He passed with honors.

Damn that child!

We all knew Christopher had the intelligence to excel and

achieve, just not the motivation. Well, at least he could say he had a high school education.

At the same time I was in counseling, I took a seventeen-year-old Christopher to a renowned child study center to see if they might be able to shed some light on his continuing difficulty in dealing with ordinary life issues. He seemed to have no sense of right or wrong. He had not acquired the normal hygienic practices most teen-agers swing into when they become interested in members of the opposite sex, and he still was living in a filthy room. We had given him the third-floor loft in our condominium to use for his computer and entertainment. It was trashed to such an extent that I wouldn't even go up there. It was simply too much for me to stomach. I guess you could say I was in deep denial, hoping by some miracle Christopher would clean it up and keep it that way.

For almost a year, the counselors at the center came up with nothing. Christopher had his own counselor, while William and I had ours. Nothing of Christopher's treatment or test results was ever shared with us. The result in 1987 was that I was treated for depression and we were told to move Christopher into his own apartment. That part I liked. His father and I paid the rent and utilities on it for two years. Christopher got a job, lived apart from us, and I didn't have to deal with him on a day-to-day basis.

In due course, Mariah moved in with Christopher and, despite birth control openly available, got pregnant and had an abortion. I was appalled, to say the least. I was also angry at Mariah for not using birth control and at Christopher for not using condoms. Were they really that stupid or naïve? I don't consider abortion to be an acceptable means of birth control. Apparently, that's exactly what it was for Mariah, fueling my growing anger and dislike of her. We learned years later she had three or four more abortions which to me was unfathomable. I was also disappointed that once again I had failed, this time by not conveying to Christopher a sense of moral responsibility for creating a life that he knew would be so carelessly aborted.

In 1988, Mariah had a full-term pregnancy that produced a lovely little boy. We first saw Michael in the hospital about three hours after he was born. Like Christopher, he was a beautiful baby, not full of redness or wrinkles, just sleeping contentedly in his bassinet next to Mariah's bed. Christopher stood by her side, beaming with the joy of being a father. We all cooed and aaahed over him, taking turns holding him. My first grandchild, I thought. I wanted to hold this little bundle forever. I wanted to spoil him the way only a grandmother can. I wanted all the best in the world for this new life, this boy who was part of me, this little guy who carried my DNA. You might say I was a proud grandma. Sadly, I think I knew my dreams would be limited.

Mariah was eighteen and Christopher was nineteen. Neither of them was capable of taking care of a baby, and neither of them wanted either set of parents to take care of the baby. I am not sure when or how the decision was made, but by the time they told us about the pregnancy, Mariah was five months pregnant. It had already been decided that the baby would be given up for adoption.

The ramifications of that decision bother me to this day. Maybe I, too, should have gotten a lawyer and fought for grandparent rights, but at the time I didn't know we needed to do that. It was supposed to be an open adoption and we, as grandparents, and Tom's mother as his great-grandmother, were assured by the adoptive parents that we would be able to visit Michael. Michael's new parents lived in Lincoln, Nebraska, while we lived on the east coast. Visits would, by geography alone, be at a minimum. We agreed to share pictures and presents, and phone calls were frequent.

All seemed to be going well until our first visit was proposed when Michael was three months old, and then the doors slammed shut. I continued to try and keep in contact with Michael by sending him gifts and cards for his birthday. At first, it was hard to figure out what to send someone you didn't know but loved. I hit upon the idea of sending snow-globes. They were gender neutral and were so varied that it wasn't difficult to find a nice one. Michael's mother always sent me a thank-you note but even after several years, only once did I ever get one from Michael. Michael's mother also sent pictures of him as he grew up, but those too dwindled as the years passed. The last picture we received was Michael's high school senior picture.

I had always hoped in my heart that when Michael turned eighteen, I could reach out and contact him, perhaps even get to meet him and establish a relationship of sorts. I really wanted to be his grandmother, the grandmother he never had and the grandmother I was never able to be. And so, about a month after his eighteenth birthday, I called him. We had a good conversation and I thought this would be the beginning of a something wonderful. When Michael graduated from high school, I sent him a check and a card that I signed, "Love, Grandma."

Shortly thereafter, I received a letter from him that literally shattered my dreams. He said I would never be his grandma, and he didn't want to have any further contact with me. He returned my check. It was as if someone had put a knife through my heart. I was so hurt I didn't even share the letter with William or Christopher. I cried for days on end, and the hurt wouldn't go away. Like a rejected lover, I decided that the best approach to healing my pain would be to simply end everything. I no longer send him cards or gifts. I still cry sometimes when I think of him.

Michael is now a young man and we haven't seen him since

his birth. He is my only biological grandchild. In 2010, Michael showed up on Facebook. Christopher friended him and suggested I send him a friend request, which I did. Michael accepted. It turned out that he looks exactly like Tom and Christopher. Exactly. I have never broached the subject of a meeting. I don't dare. I occasionally "like" one of his posts and rarely ever comment.

God always helps me out when I need it the most. In 1993, while cruising in our boat, we met a lovely young couple with two children: a boy six and a girl five. Over the years, we all fell in love with each other and we are now their Granny Rita and Granny William. Quite honestly, I do consider them to be my grandchildren and their parents to be my children. For sure, I love them as much as if I had birthed both.

Meanwhile, nine months after Michael was born, Christopher and Mariah were married in a simple ceremony at our church. We had a lovely reception for them at our home with a multitude of family and friends attending. Life went on. Although Mariah was not my ideal daughter-in-law, for some unexplainable reason, I was happy that they were getting married. I was happy that I might now have some semblance of peace again. I'm sure I even thought they might have more children and I could have a relationship with them, someone to take the place of Michael. All thoughts that Christopher was gay vanished from my mind's horizon.

WHAT NEXT?

Aahh, an empty nest. Many mothers dread it. I must admit, I loved it. With Christopher married and on his own, I concentrated on my life with William and my career. I left my corporate position after eleven years and formed my consulting firm. It probably wasn't the best career decision I could have made because I wasn't a natural born salesperson. But I desperately needed a change, and it seemed like a good move. I was never successful at it and only managed to survive for three years with good friends hiring me to help with their consulting projects. But it did take my mind off Christopher and the problems that had haunted me for years. I was ready to find normalcy in my life.

Christopher and Mariah visited for weekend meals, as did my elder daughter, Holly, and her husband, Kevin. William and I traded our sailboat in for a forty-three-foot trawler, because my back could no longer handle the rigors of sailing. I love the water, and being on the boat was the best therapy to calm my troubled heart and ease the stresses and strains of everyday life. There is something overwhelmingly mystical and magical about being out on the water. The path beneath you feels soft as a foam pillow. There is the steady rhythmic motion of the boat, not unlike the motion of a swing, more like sitting and bouncing on a large soft, rubber ball. Every once in a while, a passing boat throws out a wake and the boat rocks from side to side, not dangerously, but gently and soothingly.

The sea air, mixed as it is with crisp salt, is unlike anything on land. It is deeply invigorating, renewing, and refreshing. It has the fresh, sharp smell of a newly opened can of Fresca soda. I could breathe it in all day. Sailing, as opposed to motoring, was always much more joy. When the sails are hoisted, the engine turned off, one glides on a serene sea-road, with not a sound to interrupt or disturb one's psyche. Finally, when the anchor is set, the harbor calm, and a magnificent fiery fuchsia sunset just beginning, there is no more comforting place to be than in the cockpit or on the bridge with a glass of wine and your soulmate. And then, when the time comes to sleep, the gentle rocking of the boat assures a peaceful night.

From late May to late September, we would go out Friday night for the weekend, returning on Sunday night, refreshed and ready to face the coming week. I would have to say 1989 was as restful and rejuvenating as any since Christopher was born. It might not have been so refreshing if I knew what was to come.

In October of 1989, eleven months after the wedding, Christopher was back home, a broken young man. Life with Mariah was one affair of hers after another. When Christopher found her dallying with his best friend, he left her and came home. Once more, organized mom shifted into high gear to take care of her troubled young son. The first thing I did was cancel the lease. Christopher didn't want to stay there, not that I blame him. Next, Tom, William, and I spent days cleaning out the filth and mess that had been created over the course of the past two years.

It was an unimaginable horror. There were dirty clothes strewn over every square inch of the floor. Dirty dishes were stacked on every inch of space in the kitchen – in the sink, in the oven, in the microwave, in the freezer, on the floor, on the table, on the stove. Everywhere. There wasn't even enough room to wash the dishes without putting some in the other room. There were cigarette butts and ashes in every corner, most not even in ashtrays.

The one bedroom was in a similar state of disarray. The bed had no linens. Towels, clothes, makeup, shoes were all thrown about as if simply thrown in the dump. The place had, in fact, been turned into a disgusting, smelly, filthy landfill. We cleaned as best we could, but the landlord kept the security deposit to put it back in habitable condition. The picture of that disheveled apartment is seared on the back of my brain. This scene would not be the last such one I would encounter.

Finally, I called our attorney.

"How much for an uncontested divorce?"

He told me $900 and the wheels of divorce began grinding. In what is probably the quickest divorce on record, Christopher and Mariah were no longer a married couple within a matter of months. And within those same months, my spiritual solitude vanished as Christopher moved back into the house. There were some rules this time. At least I thought there were. I guess in retrospect, William and I should have learned from experience that rules simply don't work with Christopher.

Whenever we escaped on the boat for a weekend or went away for a weekend at an inn, there were drug parties in our home, culminating one St. Patrick's Day with a keg party for some one hundred people. At least Christopher locked most of the valuables in the master bedroom. Even then, a set of sterling silver salad forks disappeared from our sideboard. The neighbors finally told us what was going on. To the extent possible, we tried to keep Christopher under control by having him stay with his father while we were away, locking up valuables, and sadly, even restricting our travel pleasures. Rules that a normal person might think reasonable, like picking up after yourself, cleaning up the kitchen when you are done cooking, keeping a neat, clean room, or even keeping yourself clean, were generally ignored. Discipline such as withholding money, favors, or grounding were totally useless. Christopher was now an adult who should have been making his own way in the world. Instead, he was a millstone around my neck, leaving me once more frustrated and angry at this child of mine who wasn't responding to me or to life in general.

College seemed worth a try, so we enrolled Christopher in a local college. For a while, he seemed to blossom. He did well in art and photography. He proudly brought his A-graded sketches home but rarely mentioned his other classes. He had shown a talent for photography while at boarding school, and we were encouraged that maybe Christopher had found his niche. We even offered to send him to Rochester Institute of Technology for a program in photography, but he adamantly refused to go. I think he saw it as another "sending away," and in some respects, I guess I would have to agree. Our college bubble burst before the end of the first semester when, once more, Christopher was failing all his courses and rarely showing up. His old patterns had returned. In all probability, they never left. Christopher had just become more adept at manipulation and lies to cover up his behavior, and I had become more adept at denying there was any real problem. I desperately wanted my child to succeed.

"What next?" or maybe more aptly, "What now?" became my mantra. For the next year-and- a-half, Christopher was in and out of the house, either by his choice or due to our frustration and anger at his behavior as we tossed him out more than once. I remember one miserable scene when I had come home from a long, exhausting trip out west only to find Christopher up in the third-floor loft smoking pot with his friends. William was not yet home and, quite frankly, I lost it. I ran up two flights of stairs like a screaming banshee, yelling for them all to get out. I guess I kept it up for a while, because it wasn't long before the loft was cleared out and Christopher was standing there, staring at me bug-eyed.

I screamed, "GET OUT OF MY SIGHT! GET OUT OF THIS HOUSE! GO! NOW!"

With his tail between his legs, Christopher left. I didn't see him for two weeks. Thankfully, he did let us know he was staying with a friend, so I didn't have the guilt and worry that he was out somewhere getting killed.

We were told to exercise this kind of tough love with Christopher, so we did. But it didn't work. We kept laying down the rules (again and again), kicking him out of the house, constantly urging him to get a job, withholding money, trying to keep a schedule of meals, and staying as close to home as our jobs would allow. We were counseled to play a game called "Information," where you pull out topics and talk about them. It was supposed to be a way of communicating, as opposed, say, to yelling at each other. Things would calm down for a while so long as we remained vigilant. But then another flare-up would occur over something as minor as Christopher making a snide comment, and the vicious cycle would start all over again. I guess we simply weren't tough enough. Then again, maybe tough love isn't always the answer.

The only arguments William and I ever had were over Christopher and his behavior, or rather, his lack of what we considered normal behavior. Usually, William would blame Christopher for something without any real evidence or cause and I would jump to my son's defense. Or William would call him lazy or some other derogatory term. However, at the end of one of those William/Christopher matches, a particularly nasty argument occurred between us when William flung out the words that he wished Christopher had never been born.

A burst of angry fire shot through my body. At the top of my lungs, I yelled, "DON'T YOU EVER SAY THAT AGAIN! HOW DARE YOU WISH THAT MY SON WAS NEVER BORN!"

I then stormed upstairs, slammed the bedroom door, and locked it. After about one more minute of extreme fuming, I took a blanket and a pillow and threw them outside the bedroom door. William slept on the couch that night, and I cried myself to sleep. I was livid, purple, crimson livid, and I didn't get over it for many days. It still hurts me because it was the epitome of rejection of my son. No one rejects my children. No one.

As his mother, I was adamant that I would always love Christopher no matter what. At the same time, I desperately wanted him to straighten out or find out what was causing his obviously aberrant behavior. On the one hand, I knew I couldn't ever give up on him. On the other hand, I wanted to completely forget that he was ever a part of my life. I often joked with friends that if Christopher had been my firstborn, there would never have been a second.

The next thing that happened, however, was not a Christopher event.

ONE PIECE OF THE PUZZLE

It was March 21, 1991, our eleventh wedding anniversary, I flew home from my consulting assignment in Portland, Oregon, looking forward to a nice dinner at our favorite restaurant. As usual, William met me at the door, gave me a big hug and kiss, and carried my suitcase upstairs to the master bedroom. I was unusually tired, but not wanting to back out of our special dinner, I freshened up and went downstairs to enjoy a pre-dinner glass of wine on our patio overlooking the harbor. It was just about sunset and it was spectacular that night, the cirrus clouds providing the perfect canvas for the deep fuchsia light show. The mirror-glass water of the harbor reflected the pink kiss of the sun. Life, I remember thinking, doesn't get any better than this.

As I toasted our anniversary, William turned to me, put his arm around my shoulder, and in a low, quiet voice said, "I've been fired."

I was stunned. He then went on to tell me that the entire management team of his recently sold business unit had been dismissed that day, the day the two companies closed the deal. I couldn't believe it. They had been promised there would be no personnel changes. How could this be? I just sat there staring out at the harbor for what seemed like a lifetime as the sun set on our seemingly perfect life. And, then as I looked into the sadness and disappointment in William's eyes, I leaned over and just held him in my arms. We sat that way in silence until the darkness drove us inside.

Our "What now?" came about because of many nights of praying and many days of wonderings. We would sit on the patio every evening, talking over what to do next. Each of us was trying to allay the fear that dwelt in our hearts. Both being active doers, planners, and managers, it was not often that we talked about fear. But we both knew it was there. And fear's constant companion was uncertainty. There were many alternatives, but only one eventually made sense. My current consulting project was coming to an end in August of 1991. At fifty-eight, William's prospects of landing another senior executive job at the beginning of a serious recession didn't appear bright. Therefore, after about a month of pondering, we reached the decision to sell our condo in Connecticut (including most of our beautiful antique furnishings) and start over in Florida.

In May of 1990, we had purchased a small condominium on Siesta Key in Sarasota, Florida, presumably for our retirement when William reached age sixty-five, some eight years hence. It was perfect, with two little bedrooms and two baths on a small lagoon off the Intracoastal Waterway, with its own boat dock right out front. It was affordable since we had to live on our savings and a small pension from William's company. It was not an easy decision to make, but the only one that made any kind of economic sense at all. In the back of my heart, I think it was also a decision to put some distance between Christopher and us.

There was the usual flurry of activity associated with moving, but we also had the task of selling our furnishings. We interviewed several folks who made estate auctions happen, selected one, and set about deciding what, if anything, we would keep. There was only a modicum of things to take since we were moving from a 2,300 square foot home into a 1,200 square foot condo. We asked our children what, if anything, they wanted and gladly gave it to them. The rest we left up to the auctioneer to price and sell. Anything left over was sold as a lot to another dealer.

It was for me a wrenching giving up of everything. I loved our home on the harbor; I loved our wonderful antiques that we had spent days in small antique shops over the years selecting. Each day, I would wander through each room and just stand there and simply look at them all, hoping to soak everything into my memory so that they would never be entirely lost to me. To this day, I can remember each room, and I visit them often. I have a magnet on my refrigerator that says, "We never completely leave anything we love. We take a part of it with us and we leave a part of us behind with it."

I never cried. I'm much too practical to be so sentimental that it gets in the way of my better judgment. But, it was the hardest leaving I ever had to do. And yes, I did leave a part of me behind. We drive past the place every time we're in the area. On one trip, we were even bold enough to knock on the door for a look inside, but no one was home.

The day of the auction at the house, we moved onto our trawler, Empyrean (Greek for "where the gods live"). Our dock was directly in front of our townhome, so we were witness to the departing of our worldly goods. It was hard. Day by day, the house emptied as a stream of people came to pick up their purchases. I tried not to notice, but when a large van pulls up and takes out your sixteen-foot sectional sofa, it's hard to miss.

During the ensuing summer, I was back and forth to Portland to complete my work there while William was busy getting the trawler ready to take her down the Intracoastal Waterway to our new home and, I tried to tell myself, our new adventure. The trawler wasn't being cooperative, with one thing or the other breaking down as soon as one thing was prepped and made ready for the trip. Finally, the last week of August, she was ready and so were we.

The week before our departure, a neighbor had a going away party for us with friends and family. They gave us some wonderful gifts as reminders of how much they would miss us. One gift was a set of plastic tumblers replete with palm trees and flamingos. The most useful gift was a book detailing every bridge we would encounter on our voyage. The night before our departure, we had dinner on board with my children and said our goodbyes. It was not a sad occasion but one of hope as we repeatedly toasted for the future since it was a great place for the kids to visit.

August 31 was a beautiful summer morning. We left with not a soul stirring on the docks. We were alone in the early morning mist. At 7:00 a.m., we cast off the lines for the last time and backed out of the slip into the harbor where, in the early morning stillness, the water was like glass, not a ripple on the surface. Tears of sadness finally fell in small rivulets down my cheeks as I looked back at our home growing smaller and smaller in the distance.

I was suddenly filled with fear at the prospect of the 1,600-mile trip ahead of us into the unknown. Neither of us had ever been this adventurous, but I kept my feelings to myself as I took the helm and William put the lines away. It wasn't long, however, when the fear faded into the gentle rocking of the boat, and we motored down the middle of Long Island Sound under a shroud of light fog. We were completely alone. In truth, I felt very much alone and in need of some reassurance this trip and our new life would be safe and successful.

And so I prayed. I prayed that God would send me a sign that we would have a safe voyage. As my prayer ended, a large Monarch butterfly flew right in front of my eyes. It hesitated a moment, then circled twice around my head and disappeared as I steered Empyrean south. We were seven miles from any shore, and there was no land in sight. It was to be my sign each day that we would be safe. Every day of our trip, we saw a butterfly somewhere. While it was not always a Monarch, it was a butterfly. I still see butterflies as my sign from God that I will be safe. And from that moment, I relaxed. My fear dissipated and I asked William for a cup of coffee. With peace and confidence, we sailed on.

By the time we left for Florida, Christopher had taken up residence permanently with Annie, the aunt of one of his friends. We knew nothing more about her except that she was fourteen years his senior. Christopher was almost twenty-three and showed no interest in moving to Florida with us. Of course, we never really explored that possibility with him either. I know I was hoping someone else could help Christopher grow up.

In November of 1991, we reached Sarasota and lived aboard at Marina Jack's for another month while our condo tenants moved out. Each day was a new adventure for us as we explored our new environment. Having lived most of my life in the Northeast with wonderful hills and lush greenery in the summer and stark bare trees in the winter, Florida was quite the change. For one thing, it was flat. The flora and fauna were distinctly different, and although I loved the majestic palm trees, there were enough scrub brushes in the rural areas to resemble the Southwest desert. But the weather was magnificent, and it was such a joy to get up each morning to the warmth of the sun streaming in the aft window in our stateroom. Here it was in the middle of our northeastern winter and we could both put on our robes, grab a cup of coffee and head for the fly bridge to enjoy the warm weather and watch the marina activity as we planned our day. Our boat slip was some ways out into the harbor, so we had an unobstructed view of the bay.

While we had many practical things to do like furniture shopping, we always planned what we came to call a "discovery" trip. There were so many new places and new things to explore. Each day, we tried to discover something new: a museum, a new beach, the swamps, a new restaurant (there were many), or even a new shopping center. As it turned out, even buying new furniture was an adventure, as we had to decide on wicker or oak, blue or white fabric, an entertainment center, or TV table, a glass table or not, chairs with casters or not, all the things that make up putting a home together. We eventually settled on wicker, glass, light colors, and anything tropical, since it seemed to go with our beach environment.

On our discovery jaunts, we explored our new neighborhood, walking the beach at sunset, eating at a local eatery, or just driving around looking and going nowhere in particular. We considered each day a new adventure. I once remarked that it felt like we were a pair of newlyweds setting up our first home in a foreign land.

While we had a thrilling and exhilarating trip down the Intracoastal Waterway in our trawler without any major mishaps, we were eagerly looking forward to this new chapter of our life together. Having left two cars behind, we asked Christopher to drive one car down to us. He arrived on Thanksgiving Day.

Sometime during that weekend, Christopher and I were alone in the main cabin. William had gone to bed, and we were just chatting about inconsequential things. How was the trip down in the car? Was his job installing sun-roofs going well? How was Annie? It was windy that evening, and the waves in the harbor were slapping gently on the sides of the boat. It was almost like a tribal drum beat: regular, quietly soothing. The cabin of our trawler was a nice size with a banquette wrapping around the starboard side. Opposite was a comfortable easy chair with a table and lamp next to it. A large kerosene trawler lamp hung over a low coffee table positioned in front of the banquette, casting off a warm glow. I loved how it shed just the right amount of light in the cabin, and I used it as our main source of light whenever I could. Christopher's slender frame was stretched out on the banquette with his hair slightly ruffled since he had recently awakened from a nap. I was sitting in the easy chair opposite, where I often sat to read in the evening. The boat was rocking gently with the wind.

After a brief lull in our conversation, Christopher said in a rather low, secretive kind of voice, "Mom, do you remember when I was sixteen and told you I had a secret that I couldn't tell anyone?"

Remember? You bet! My ears perked up, I sat straight up in my chair, leaned forward, and wondered if this was that big reveal moment I had been anticipating. It struck me that although I really wanted to know his secret, I was also somewhat apprehensive about what it might be and the consequences it might have on our lives. Christopher then said, "Mom, I'm a cross dresser."

"Really?"

"Yeah, mom. I am. I've been dressing in women's clothes for years."

"Hmmm, I didn't know. How does Annie feel about it?" I asked.

How banal. Shouldn't I be saying something brilliant, or supportive?

"Oh, she's fine with it. In fact, I have more ladies' clothes than she does. We have a blast shopping for outfits."

Oh my, well at least one of my suspicions was right. I didn't say anything more for a few minutes as I picked up our dessert dishes, retreated to the galley, and asked Christopher if he wanted a cup of coffee. Quite frankly, I didn't know what else to say. It's one thing to think something about someone or something and then to find out it's true. My heart sank, and I knew I had to say something more.

Finally, I decided this was not an end to the world. Since most cross dressers did so in private, it wouldn't really impact us. Yet I wished it weren't the case. Or maybe I wished I didn't know something so personal and private about my son. I finally asked Christopher what it was like to be a cross dresser. It opened the door for further conversation. A couple of glasses of wine helped, and we could talk a lot that evening about Christopher's cross dressing and even about the possibility he was gay.

"Mom, I'm not gay. I've told you that before. I just love to dress in women's clothes. I love the way they feel on my skin, especially the feel of silk blouses and underwear."

I giggled. "Yes, I always like the way my silk blouses feel too."

"I'm not cross dressing in public, you know. You don't have to worry about my embarrassing you."

What a huge relief. At least I didn't have to worry if one of my friends were to see him traipsing down the street or dining in a restaurant.

"That's a relief," I managed to choke out.

As the evening ended, we hugged and said our good-nights. Christopher headed to the forward cabin and me to the aft cabin, where William was sound asleep, gently snoring. As I was unbuttoning my blouse, taking off my slacks, and slipping into my nightgown, I felt this huge cloud of doubt and unrest. It was as if I wanted to accept his cross dressing, but at the same time didn't want to. It was such a confusing set of feelings. I felt that Christopher had shared his secret with me, but I wasn't happy about it. That bothered me. I knew I should support my son, but that didn't seem to come easily. I hardly slept all night.

After Christopher had left to go back to Annie, with his permission, I told William about our evening conversation. William is a stoic and faces every situation with an outwardly surreal calm. I saw the surprise reflected in his eyes, but his words didn't mirror that emotion. His comments were, "Well, okay" and "It isn't something I would do, but we know it is something some people do."

Really? Oh, sure. But, hey it's not your kid.

As a stepparent, William brought a sense of objectivity into the conversation. It really wasn't the end of the world. If Christopher weren't out there parading around in public as a woman, then what was the harm? It was something he would do in private. Eventually, after days that seemed like years of discussing the subject, we realized it was almost a relief to have an answer to one part of the puzzle that was Christopher, even if cross dressing wasn't a lifestyle we would choose for ourselves. But in my heart, I believed there was something much more.

And I was right.

Christopher, 1969

Christopher, 1971

Christopher, 1974

Spectrum

Family, Fashion and Lifestyle

The Trumbull Times, Thursday, November 13, 1980

Christopher, 1980

Christopher, Summer 1980

Christopher, 1982

Christopher, Rita, William 1985

Tom, Christopher, 1991

Christopher/Wendy, 1993

Christopher, 1995

Christopher, 1993

Kristen, 2001

Kristen, 2001

Kristen, 2003

Kristen, 2004

Kristen, 2005

ANNIE

It was an immense burden lifted off my shoulders with Annie now taking care of Christopher. And I knew it was truly a "taking care of" situation. With her fourteen-year's seniority, however, we all agreed that in many respects, Christopher had gravitated to her as another mother figure. That was just fine as far as I was concerned. Someone else was now struggling with getting him up in the morning, or keeping his room clean, or taking a shower, or finding (and keeping) a job. Someone else was worrying about whether he might be dead or alive at 3:00 a.m. Someone else was worrying about just about everything Christopher paid no heed to, and that was a mighty big job. I relaxed – an older, more mature woman was at the helm.

We didn't meet Annie for another year and a half until 1993, when they drove down from Connecticut to spend a week with us. I really didn't know what to expect, because Christopher never really gave us any indication of who Annie was, what she looked like, what she liked or didn't like. What Christopher had told me was they were a couple now and she was his significant other. I am not the kind of person who makes a judgment about someone until I have met him or her. I was, however, ready to meet the woman who was tending to the needs of my son. I wanted to thank her and I hoped we would forge a good relationship and both work together for the benefit of my son.

When Annie walked in the door to our condo, I was astonished. She was tall, about 5'10" I would guess, dressed in a flowing, loose, floor length hippie-type, multi-colored dress. She had long brown hair flowing down nearly to her waist with an artificial flower tucked behind one ear, and she was adorned with multiple rings, bracelets, and necklaces. But what really shocked me was she was a big woman, all three hundred-plus pounds of her. And she was a plain woman, not pretty, with what appeared to be a permanent frown etched into her brow. Annie was not the physically attractive woman I had always envisioned my son would choose for a partner. I showed them to their room with a smile pasted on my face and decided to simply be gracious and get through the week. It wasn't easy, and I think the insides of my cheeks still bear the scars from biting them to keep silent and remain pleasant. It would be better when I got to know her, I thought.

We took them to the John and Mabel Ringling Museum, out to brunch, lunch and dinner, a boat ride on the gulf, and generally tried to give them an enjoyable time. Like a couple of light-hearted young lovers, laughing, holding hands, giggling, they spent days at the pool or on the crystal white sands of Siesta Key Beach, one of the best in the world. It was quite apparent they were happy together. Annie and I spent hours talking. She shared her childhood stories and some of her young adult traumas with me. She shared her book of poetry with me because I was a writer and had a column published biweekly in the local newspaper, and she wanted my opinion. She shared her struggles with Christopher and her acceptance of his cross dressing. Living with Christopher was a challenge for Annie and, like the rest of us, she thought she was dealing with someone she could "shape up." She even threatened to "ship him out" if he didn't shape up, she told me. I knew that would never happen. You see, for Annie, being in love with a much younger, quite handsome young man was way too much an aphrodisiac for her to want him out of her life. Christopher fed her ego and she literally kept him sheltered, clothed, fed, and I presume, sexually satisfied.

Annie followed me around that week like a new puppy looking for attention, reassurance, or acceptance. She was always trying to help around the house, asking me for my opinions on a variety of subjects, and apologizing if she thought she said or did something wrong. It became clear to me after a few days that Annie needed my acceptance. Of course, I was the mother-in-law figure. I was pleasant, but guarded. While I could see her as a caretaker for my son, I was less enthusiastic about her being his lover and even less enthusiastic about her possibly becoming his wife. These thoughts were troubling. As a mother, I knew I should be happy my child had found someone to love and share life with. But I guess with the age difference, her unattractiveness, and her neediness, I just couldn't accept the thought of a lifetime with her as a daughter-in-law.

She talked incessantly about getting married. I tried to caution her about Christopher's instability, but I knew that wasn't about to slow her down for one minute. In private, Christopher told me that he was never going to marry again, and that included Annie. I guess that made me relax somewhat, but I've learned through the years that sometimes what people vow will happen often doesn't happen, and vice versa. I've also learned never to say never and never to say always.

I have often wondered if my feelings about Annie were just a knee-jerk, mother-type reaction to losing a son or something else. Deep in my mother's heart is the need to be sure that no one hurts Christopher. Deep inside my psychic soul, however, I have this ever-darkening sense that Christopher will never be able to stand alone against the world. It is that fear that drives me to try and find all the puzzle pieces and put them together. I knew that I was going to depend on Annie to help me find them.

Over the ensuing years, Annie and I would often talk on the

phone about Christopher. I knew the frustrations she was going through with him, because I had walked that walk. Because of her ever-deepening love for him, she too struggled with finding the puzzle pieces and packaging them to make a whole, responsible, mature adult out of him. I think it was probably Annie who first recognized that he might always be just who he was - Christopher – living in the space of today with no consequence of his past guiding him, nor any sense of the future motivating him. He was living in a space I call today. For Christopher, it seems to always be today, and to try looking or acting or moving into or out of anything different is difficult, if not impossible. At least that is how I experience Christopher.

Christopher and Annie were in Florida on another visit in the fall of 1995. I think we flew them down and let them use one of our cars. On this trip, they weren't the same light-hearted young lovers as they were on the first visit in 1993. Annie was quieter, sullen, not as talkative, and certainly more demanding, ordering Christopher to wait on her hand and foot. She would pick an argument over something as small as whether he opened the car door for her or helped her sit down at the table. Even the permanent frown on her face was somehow darker, deeper, more foreboding. She wasn't as friendly toward me, and I wondered if it was something I said or did. This turnaround in behavior left me puzzled and wondering why.

Remember Wendy from the first chapter? Something was brewing with Annie and Christopher and that something was "Wendy," the cross dresser. In fact, as we know, it was Wendy, the transgender male-to-female. Over their time together I am sure it was a frequent topic of discussion. Annie, no doubt, was the first to know, and may even have been the first to suspect the truth of Christopher's sexual orientation. In fact, the night we learned of it, Annie said it didn't surprise her in the least.

Oh, really? Why?

She then described all the female traits she saw in him – the swish of his walk, the flick of his hand, the purse of his lips, the feminine tilt of his head, things I never noticed in the twenty-plus years of his life. But, why would I? To me, he was my son, not my daughter. There are so many days that I wish Wendy was a real tropical storm rather than the emotional hurricane of sexual orientation that it was for us. I can honestly say the evening Christopher told us he wanted to be, excuse me, *was* a woman, changed us all forever.

Over the ensuing months, Annie and I discussed many of the ramifications of what this would mean in both of their lives, Christopher was not ready to come out, as it were, to the rest of the family, the family being primarily his father, sister, and grandmother. We promised that we wouldn't breathe of a word of this to anyone. After all, it really wasn't for us to tell, although

I often wonder if Christopher wouldn't have preferred for us to run interference for him with his father and sister who, he was certain, simply wouldn't understand or support him. Our lips were sealed, and thus Christopher's secret remained one only to be spoken of within the confines of our small family circle of four.

With each phone call over the following years, there were conversations about how Christopher was dealing with his gender issues and what progress he had made. Apparently, he was in that phase when the reality of becoming the other gender was a scary place, and he would vacillate from one day to the next.

Should I? Shouldn't I? Is this real?

He would be losing one identity to become another. What would it be like? Was he ready to come out to all? Had he changed his mind completely? Was he still unsure? Of course, his uncertainty added fuel to our uncertainty as to how to handle the situation. For once, though. we were wise, kept quiet, and let him be the leader.

THE BAHAMA MAMA

In June of 1996, I was headed off to seminary and three years of study towards ordination to the Episcopal priesthood. Quite a change from corporate duty, property management, and writing columns about condominiums. I was quite surprised by the strength and insistence of this call, but I knew it was what God was calling me to do now for some reason. But, that's a whole other book. I will say that neither William nor Christopher were in the least surprised by my call. Christopher even told me I had a very strong spiritual energy surrounding me.

By this time, Christopher and Annie were preparing to move to Dallas, where his father, Tom, had relocated from Connecticut the previous year. This move prompted me to wonder if it were possible Christopher had to be always near one or the other of his parents. Without our fully grasping it, I believe Tom and I were his final support system if all else failed.

We sold our condo in Siesta Key and took our boat back up the waterway to Washington, DC, to live aboard her at the Capital Yacht Club while I attended seminary in Virginia. As a gift to ourselves, we decided to take a side trip to the Bahamas on the way up. We invited Christopher and Annie to go with us.

Annie's birthday was the fourteenth of June, which also happens to be our church wedding anniversary. We were docked at the Green Turtle Club in the Abacos and had planned a festive meal to celebrate both events. The day began with everyone smiling, languishing in the breeze that lightly ruffled the cabin curtains, downing our bagels, lox, cream cheese, and capers. After breakfast, we headed to the inviting salt water pool, swam a bit, snacked a bit, and slathered each other with SPF 15 to keep from burning. Christopher was grinning and laughing as he and Annie splashed and dunked each other in the pool. I was content to lie back in a lounge chair, soak up some rays, or read a chapter or two of whatever book I was reading. William spent a good deal of time floating in the pool or sleeping in the chair beside me.

Lunch was some island treat at the poolside Tiki bar. I can't remember what I ate, but I do remember the delicious Bahama Mamas, a potent island drink so good we practically inhaled them. A few specks of squishy white clouds sauntered overhead. As the day wore on it promised to be a delightful, balmy evening. The prevailing easterly softly caressed our cheeks. The hot morning temperatures gradually dropped.

Around 4:00 p.m. Annie and Chris went off exploring the island as I headed back to the boat to prepare dinner. Groceries are very expensive in the islands, so every spare inch of space in the galley and cabin was crammed with food purchased before we departed. On hands and knees, I retrieved some yummy marinated artichokes and pita chips from behind the settee drawers, which were level with the floor. I mixed them with some herbs and mayonnaise for a nice appetizer dip, and turned to fetching the ingredients for the main meal. From our freezer, I selected the prime rib-eye steaks, a fitting entrée for two such celebrations. Since we had only been at sea for a couple of weeks, I still had enough fresh romaine to make a crisp Caesar salad. William returned from the pool around 5:00 p.m. and mixed his extraordinary Caesar dressing while I set the table. To make it a bit more special, I walked out onto the dock toward the clubhouse and cut a few Hibiscus I found hugging the shoreline for my centerpiece. The table looked so festive, and I was in an extremely good mood.

We all changed into our nicest clothes for cocktails on the fly bridge. Annie and I each chose a floral print muumuu to wear accessorized with bangles and beads. William and Christopher each wore a Hawaiian print shirt and shorts. We were all barefoot and suntanned like my Starbucks mocha latte. Together, we were a rainbow of vibrancy. It was so relaxing that we spent hours on the bridge chatting, drinking, laughing, and nibbling as the boat rocked side to side from the gentle wakes of passing boats. The smile on Christopher's face and the loving looks exchanged with Annie made me realize how happy he was at this moment. I reached over and held William's hand as we sat in awed silence, enchanted by one of the most beautiful fuchsia-splashed sunsets I've ever seen.

During dinner in the main salon, classical music played softly in the background as the glow of our large kerosene trawler lamp wrapped its warmth around us. Our evening was full of joyful champagne toasts to each other for future years of birthdays and anniversaries. Crusty on the outside, pink on the inside, our steaks were grilled to perfection. Caesar would have been proud of the salad festooned with homemade croutons, lightly coated with William's special dressing. We capped off the meal with coffee from fresh ground beans and a fudgy Devil's food cake with a dollop of vanilla ice cream.

There was no moon that evening, but lights from the docks twinkled on the water. We could occasionally hear laughter wafting across the water from other boats either slipped or anchored in the harbor. As other boaters walked past our festive affair, we would wave and say "Good evening." Boating people have an ease and approachability about them I've not found in other specialized communities. It was a real celebration. Happy birthday. Happy anniversary.

As often happens at family gatherings when there is excessive drinking, an argument broke out between William and Christopher as we were clearing the table. I cannot recall all the details, but I do remember that it was a silly disagreement between them, one of those differences of opinion where one declares that something is red and the other says it is blue. It was one of those "No, I'm right" and "No, you're wrong, I'm right." dialogs where no one would budge.

In those days there was no Google to look up answers and settle the matter. Brows furrowed, teeth pursed, fists clenched, eyes glared across the cabin, Christopher and Annie stomped off the boat. I left too and walked around the now deserted docks for a bit. I needed to calm myself down.

These encounters always sent me into a hot rage, wondering why two adults could so quickly turn into five-year-old boys. No matter how I bellowed, beat upon their psyches, or pitched out nasty adjectives on their unhearing ears, it didn't stop them. Would I ever learn to simply walk away and let them have at each other? After about an hour of pacing up and down, cooling down, I returned to find William had cleaned up our dinner dishes and was getting ready for bed. By 11:00 p.m., the kids weren't back yet and we went to bed thinking they were probably at the club enjoying the music.

I was awakened at 1:30 a.m. by William gently shaking me,

"Christopher and Annie want to tell you something."

With eyes barely open, I grabbed my robe, threw it over my shoulders, rubbed my eyes, and sleepily climbed the three ladder steps into the main cabin.

"What's up?" I asked.

"Mom, I've asked Annie to marry me."

My knees buckled slightly as I fought to keep my balance. Annie and Christopher just stood there in the middle of the cabin holding hands, grinning from ear to ear, giggling like two love-sick teenagers. William turned his back on us to stare out the cabin window into the dark shadows of night.

"What? Are you out of your mind? You haven't even sorted out your gender issues."

"It doesn't matter. If he decides to live as a woman, I'll stay with him. I love him," said Annie as she twisted the many rings on her fingers.

"Doesn't matter?" I squeaked. "Of course, it matters. It…it…," I stuttered, "is the most important thing in both of your lives. You need time, and until Christopher decides to continue to be a male or transition to a female, I just think it is inappropriate."

I could feel the anger rising, my mouth full of cotton, my lips twitching. I kept swallowing as if I was forcing this subject into my bowels to disappear forever. An awkward silence like an unwanted fog fell over us.

Christopher and Annie broke through the shroud and said, "We want your blessing," almost in unison, eyes searching mine, waiting for my nod of approval.

Oh, God, how can this be? This is going to be a disaster.

Christopher was holding Annie closer now, and he kept biting his lip and rocking gently as if it would calm him down.

"I'm not going to bless a marriage that I don't believe is the right thing for either of you and maybe never will be," I blurted out. "I just can't."

They stormed off the boat like an unexpected bolt of lightning for the second time. I suppose I could have been more tactful, but it was 2:00 a.m. I threw a desperate glance at William, who just looked down at his feet. I wanted to get his acceptance of this whole episode, of my position, but no words came. I spun around, went back down the ladder steps, and crawled into bed wishing it were the next afternoon and I could drown myself in Bahama Mamas.

The next day was quiet, to say the least. Breakfast was full of that nonsensical small talk about the weather, no one really looking at anyone, everyone stiff, awkward, and giving off the smell of wanting to be anywhere else. Annie noisily cleaned up the dishes. Tossing me an intense glare over her shoulder, she excused herself to go into the forward cabin to get dressed.

William said, “I’m going to find the dock master to settle up our bill so we can get underway.”

At last some precious time to be alone with Christopher.

“Now that we are all sober, are you sure you want to marry Annie? I thought you said you were never going to marry her?”

“Mom, I’ve been living with Annie for five years, and I feel as if I should marry her. She deserves it.”

“Oh my dear child, that is no reason to get married. What about your struggle to sort out your gender issues, your sexuality?”

“Annie says that when I transition to a female, we’ll live as a lesbian couple. I have to believe her.”

I just shook my head in disbelief. “Is that what you want? To live as a lesbian?”

“I’m not sure Mom. I don’t know. I’m still sorting through all my feelings and where I want to be in my life. But I am going to marry Annie.”

“Well, will you at least have a long engagement and give yourself time to think this through?”

“I only asked her to marry me last night, so it will be a while before we actually get married. Mom, your blessing is important to me, so will you please think about it?”

I nodded. Putting his hands on his knees, he pushed himself up off the cabin settee, brushed off the back of his pants, and without another word, headed into the cabin with Annie.

I sighed, refolded my napkin, put away the placemats, and centered the vase of flowers on the small teak dining table. As I gazed out the window on the quiet beauty of the harbor, I was silently hoping that if I withheld my blessing it would delay what I considered to be a disastrous union. I knew I couldn't prevent it, but given enough time, perhaps they might reconsider and see that marriage was only the answer to Annie's yearnings to be loved, not to Christopher's gender issues. In fact, it might even make them worse.

The marriage proposal was never discussed again for the rest of the trip. We switched off that pronouncement as if the conversation never happened. With pasted on smiles and courteous voices, life went on. We all tried to make the remaining voyage as fun and pleasant as possible, but we knew it was clouded by that announcement. The subject was brought up again on May 23, 1998, my fifty-ninth birthday.

FAST FORWARD

From June of 1996, to May of 1998, life progressed without much upheaval on any front. Christopher and Annie never brought up the subject of their marriage again. They both got jobs in Dallas, and Christopher enrolled in the Dallas Institute of Fine Arts and obtained his AA Degree in Computer Animation and Multimedia Art. There was no further mention of his gender issue and no one asked. I was too busy getting my Master of Divinity degree at Virginia Theological Seminary, and Christopher was too busy trying to be a man.

William and I were off to Israel for the month of May with a group from the seminary. The morning of my birthday, May twenty-third, the phone rang in our room at St. George's College. I had just stepped out of the shower and was getting ready for Sunday worship services. Getting a phone call in Israel was highly unusual, so my first thought was someone had died or was in some kind of trauma.

"Hello?" I said with that fearful questioning tone when one is expecting bad news.

"We want to wish you Happy Birthday, Mom."

"Why thank you! What a wonderful surprise. How are you both doing? Are you enjoying Dallas?"

"Mom, Annie and I are getting married tomorrow, and we want your blessing."

Well, there it was. I knew it would come one day, but the timing sucked. On my birthday. Really? A day to remember.

Christopher told me he had resolved his gender issues, and this marriage was what he wanted. After more than seven years of taking care of Christopher, I figured Annie probably did deserve the sanctity of marriage. We gave them our blessing and Tom's second wife, Alicia, a Unity minister, married them at the local Renaissance Fair in Dallas. Deep down, I knew that the gender issue had not been fully resolved. But when you are half a world away, there isn't much hope of having any meaningful dialog on the subject. Of course, Tom and Alicia had no idea there even was an issue, so we couldn't talk to them about what was happening. And so it was that Annie Logan became Annie Nelson.

Christmas Eve 1998 was spent with the entire extended family, including Tom and his wife, at the home of his mother, *Grosmutter* (German for Grandma), as the children called her. She and I had always remained close in spite of the divorce, and Tom and I had long since gotten over the hurt and anger our divorce generated. *Grosmutter* lived in the small town of Briarcliff, NY, on the Hudson River. She was ninety-one-years-old, nearly blind, hunched over so much I wondered how she managed to see anything but the floor. She was being cared for by a Romanian girl, Nadia, who lived with her. In her youth, Claire (her given name) was a tall, striking woman with a prominent streak of gray hair cascading from her forehead back to the crown of her head. While she lived in America for over seventy years, she still had a slight Swiss accent.

Holly and her husband drove down from Connecticut and Tom and Alicia flew in from Dallas, as did Christopher and Annie. We drove up from D.C. The living room was festooned with a small table-top Christmas tree in the front bay window, and a smattering of Hummel Christmas figures dotted the nearby tables. The room was not as decorated with as many items as in years long past simply because Claire was not up to the task, but the air sparkled with the many candles she used to brighten up her rooms.

As was our usual tradition, we shared cocktails and appetizers for at least two hours before any thought of dinner was expected. The joy of the season was dampened by the thought that this might be *Grosmutter's* last Christmas. Our laughter and our toasts to each other for a Merry Christmas and a Happy New Year blotted out the tarnish of that thought, at least for the next several hours. Claire sat in "her" Windsor wing chair that we sometimes called "The Throne," for she was the queen of her universe. We mingled easily together, almost as if we truly were a natural family.

Christopher was dressed in a nice three-piece suit with a Christmas tie, and Annie wore a glittering loose gown of varying colors of red in an abstract pattern. She looked pretty. The only uneasy part of the evening for me was keeping the secret of Christopher's gender struggles, knowing no one else knew, and having to remind myself constantly not to bring up the subject. Having him dressed in such strong male fashion helped me avoid the topic. In fact, it somehow bolstered the idea in my head that this whole issue had been resolved and Christopher would remain Christopher, not turn into Wendy.

I am certain that we all drank a bit too much, because we always drank too much when visiting *Grosmutter.* I'm not sure why, except her expectations of us were always so high, and it was the only way we could loosen our tongues enough to have a relaxed conversation and enjoy ourselves. We didn't worry if we would say the wrong thing or make a comment she didn't like. And this time, I was more fearful that either William or I might spill the secret beans, but we sailed through the evening without a slip.

It turned out to be a grand evening, filled with lots of conversation, laughter, and food.

"Remember the time Papa (Claire's long-deceased spouse) went for an airplane ride and wound up in Oyster Bay?"

"Remember my first smorgasbord when all I would eat were the meatballs?"

"Remember the Christmas when five-year old Cousin Johnny threw a fit because he didn't get the present he wanted?" All were "Remembers" with not a single "Next year" remark.

Although she was Swiss-born, Claire always had a Swedish smorgasbord on Christmas Eve, as dictated by Papa who was of Swedish descent. Her table was filled with every imaginable Nordic treat: head cheese, meatballs, potatoes in a cream sauce, beets, some strange fish called lutefisk, and, of course, herring in sour cream. Dessert was a tasty fruitcake with a liberal douse of liquor drizzled on top and a side of ice cream. We ate and ate and ate.

At that exact moment, as the meal ended, bellies full, faces glowing, life was good. If the world had been peeking in our window, they would have seen what appeared to be a Norman Rockwell family enjoying the holidays. But there wouldn't be another such Christmas Eve family gathering. *Grosmutter* Claire died in April of 2000.

Annie was diagnosed with multiple sclerosis in the spring of 1999, just as I graduated from seminary and was ordained as a

Deacon. Not long after Annie's diagnosis, they moved to Connecticut to be near Tom, who had retired in Massachusetts the previous year, and Annie's father and son, who lived nearby. My suspicion about Christopher's need for a parental safety-net was validated. I can honestly say that I was somewhat relieved, because I knew Christopher would need help with Annie. If they were in Dallas, none of us would be close enough to be there for them.

December of 1999 was another time for celebration, as I was ordained a priest on December 12, and a week-long party ensued at our new home in Oldsmar, Florida. Christopher and Annie flew down to join the festivities, along with my eldest daughter, Holly, and my brother from California. I loved having family with me for this special sacramental rite. Over the years, I have found at such special times, negative events or people in one's life get relegated to the shadows of a cabinet corner, sitting, waiting to come out, like the once or twice a year sterling silver bowls. Not interfering, just there. For later.

Whatever Christopher's gender orientation, whatever his narcolepsy, whatever his ADD, he and Annie were making a life together. Although they struggled living on one salary, Christopher had a good job at a photo store and Annie was getting good medical care. Her MS, though, was progressive. Within a short period, she became almost totally incapacitated.

We didn't live close enough to visit Annie and Christopher, but we did have regular telephone conversations that gave us a vague idea of what life was like for them. Within a year, Annie was confined to an electric wheelchair, unable to walk, which meant Christopher was now responsible for keeping himself, Annie, and the house together and functioning. Annie required regular visits for MRI scans and occasional visits to the ER if she had an episode of numbness or pain.

Eventually, Christopher was even taking care of Annie's hygiene, changing her diapers, bathing her, and moving her from the wheelchair to the bed they had moved from the second-floor bedroom to the living room. I don't know how he even managed to move her massive body, but he did. In addition to the added work at home, he managed to keep up with his full-time job. As months passed, I could hear the weariness creeping into his voice, and I wondered how much longer he could carry this load. I must say though, he showed more responsibility and maturity than we ever dreamed he was capable of.

And then there was March of 2000. I was at a diocesan seminar about something I can't even remember now when I received the call from Christopher early one evening that changed all our lives forever.

SECRETS

Secrets were always an integral part of our family. Some secrets are so minor one might wonder why we bother keeping them. Others are huge. We keep huge secrets. For five years as an adult, Christopher lived minutes from his father but light years away from really sharing his life secret with him. As to Christopher's gender orientation, Tom was clueless. CW, as he called Christopher, was his "son" and, although he had failed to live up to Tom's expectations, he was, after all, carrying on the Nelson name, and that was all important.

The first call came in on my cell phone. Since I was at a remote conference center in Florida, cell phone reception was spotty, so I was crouched in a dusty corner of my room so as not to drop the call.

"Mom," Christopher asked, "Have you ever told Dad about Wendy?"

"No, I haven't. That's something you have to tell him."

"Well, Mom, I decided I am going to live as a woman for the rest of my life."

Silence.

"Uh…er" clearing my throat, "are you sure?"

"Yes. Why do you always question me?"

I could hear the pain in his voice.

Oh, I don't know, maybe because you vacillate so much, lie so much, go back and forth so much, and won't tell anyone but me, William, and Annie.

Mercifully, I kept my thoughts to myself.

What I said really doesn't matter. Christopher had finally come to terms with his gender identity and had taken steps to make it more a reality than a dream or a secret. He was ready to tell his father. That step alone made me realize Christopher was serious. Perhaps by telling Tom, it meant he was ready to move forward as a woman and never look back. I told him I would support whatever decision he made, although I sensed going forward everyone's lives would be changed.

I don't think any of us suspected how difficult this transition would be. It was still a concept, not a reality. What swims around in your head as a distant concept can be shoved to the back and forgotten for a while. When it stands and stares you in the face as a real person, it can't be pushed into the dark recesses of one's mind. Not ever.

I expected the second phone call. Two days later Tom called me, appalled that we knew this secret long before he did. Thus started a series of phone calls, visits, arguments, tears, laughter, ups and downs on an emotional roller coaster that none of us was ready to ride. There were so many questions to answer, so many life changes to be made. Christopher started by throwing out all his male clothes and entering a program of psychoanalysis and discernment at a transgender clinic. He was on the way to becoming the "she" he always was. He no longer had to keep a secret.

While William and I knew years earlier about his sexuality/gender complexities, it was never real until that first phone call. We were still trying to make sense of this phenomena, filled with uncertainties and questions. When a concept becomes a reality, that reality can be intensely problematic. At least it was for me. My son becoming a woman was going to require a lot of adjustment. It was now my turn to keep it a secret, as I was not ready to announce this enormous change of circumstances to my friends and distant family. I feared they wouldn't understand or would ask questions I couldn't answer. I feared most that our family would be rejected or ostracized because of it.

We read the excellent book, *True Selves,* by Mildred L. Brown and Chloe Ann Rounsley, which Christopher recommended. It was a godsend and one of the first books on the subject that gave us an intellectual understanding of what it meant to be transgender. It even went into all the historical details of the condition and the surgeries involved, but it didn't really deal with the psychological impact on families or friends. While Christopher had made his decision to live as a woman, we were still digesting the little we had learned. I would have liked to have been able to say, "How wonderful," but I wasn't quite there yet. I still had serious doubts this was real and not some phase. I know William and Tom did too.

Annie was determined to keep her marriage together, whatever it took. I questioned whether it would. Here again, for Annie, it was only a concept at this point, not a fact. Time would only tell if this relationship could be sustained, particularly in light of the fact that Annie's MS continued to worsen. I think, and this is pure conjecture, she had no place to go, no place to hide. She needed Christopher under any circumstances to take care of her. I never had a conversation with her about it, because almost all my conversations were with Christopher. Annie and I rarely spoke.

Tom was sure that Christopher wasn't serious. Tom didn't want it to be true. Christopher's sister, Holly, had an inquiring mind. In an effort to understand, she took Christopher out to dinner from time to time, where they had lengthy conversations about his gender identity. William and I, well, we looked for books to really understand this thing called a transgender person. There wasn't much in 2000 to learn other than the technicalities of the surgery. There were only a couple of dozen books on the subject. Since I wasn't aware of the Internet for anything other than email and Google didn't exist, my ability to research the subject was limited. Those who were transgender were still sorting it out themselves and hadn't yet written all the personal accounts one finds in print and in cyberspace today. Amazon, in 2016 has more than 13,000 books listed under Transgender.

It would have been nice to have volumes to read on the subject after that first phone call, after the big reveal, but we learned more about what it means to be transgender from Christopher himself in those early years. We learned some babies are born physically with both sex organs and require surgery to become one sex or the other. Some babies are born with one physical sex and the opposite psychological sex. These children live with this dichotomy until they can come out and present themselves to the world as their psychological gender. No one knows what causes this gender dysphoria. It has been posited that perhaps this happens during a hormone wash in utero at five weeks. It wasn't until early 2015 that Boston University Medical Center reported:

The researchers conducted a literature search and reviewed articles that showed positive biologic bases for gender identity. These included disorders of sexual development, such as penile agenesis, neuroanatomical differences, such as grey and white matter studies, and steroid hormone genetics, such as genes associated with sex hormone receptors. They conclude that current data suggests a biological etiology for transgender identity.

We are still on the cusp of research into this condition. Today, we even have *I Am Cait*, a reality show on the transition of Bruce Jenner from a male to a female. Transgender is a hot topic today but Kristen isn't sure it's helpful. She thinks putting the spotlight on the condition only highlights the fact they are different, rather than helping them assimilate into the sexual gender they are regardless of physical attributes.

When one reveals a secret, especially such a big one, timing can be everything. For me, this revelation came at a particularly difficult time in my life. About one week after learning of Christopher's decision, I was told that my church position as Curate could no longer be funded. Anyone who has lost a position and needs to find another one knows how stressful that search process can be. But it had to be done, and so it was that I started what turned out to be an eight-month search for a call to another Episcopal church. Some days, I felt like I was riding two roller-coasters: one named Christopher, the other the rest of my life. I was straddled between them as one went up and the other went down, pulling at my psyche, bringing on waves of fear for my child's future, fear for the stability of my marriage, my vocation, and at times, my very sanity. But primarily, I was fearful for Christopher's future as a woman in a man's body.

My children give me great pain and heartbreak. If they're not thriving, I am in soulful pain with worry for their welfare. Some days, the pain of coping simultaneously with Christopher and the job search stretched the limits of my endurance. Some evenings, I would drown myself in wine. We topped the charts on the uncertainty scale. But with amazing grace, we moved forward. Our faith grounded us, and our daily prayers brought us a sense of peaceful holiness in an otherwise challenging atmosphere.

During this time, it might have helped if our family had been getting the same therapy as Christopher, who was receiving intense counseling about the ramifications of his transition. At one point, I even looked for a transgender counseling resource or organization and found none in our area. For me, and perhaps everyone else, we had to accept that it was therapy enough at the time just to have this secret "un-secreted." We were no longer in the position of pretending that Christopher was Christopher anymore, of keeping a secret. At least we could all talk about it openly, and talking things out is how I often work things through in my life.

A CELEBRATION OF LIFE

It is time in this story to refer to Christopher as "she." Christopher is dead. Wendy is alive in his body. I have dried three decades of tears as I keep telling myself this obvious fact. He/she is not dead. He is changed to a "she." Yes, a big deal. Yes, not an easy adjustment. The concept that a person might have one biological gender and another psychological gender was hard for me to wrap my head around. My emotions are still all over the place as to whether I have fully accepted this change: some days yes, some days not so much, some days no. I want to be that totally supportive, accepting mother, but sometimes it just didn't happen. I want to be happy that while I lost a son, I gained a daughter.

As I reflect on that time almost sixteen years ago, when I was struggling to understand gender dysphoria, I now realize I hadn't said a final goodbye to Christopher. I wish we had had a funeral for Christopher, although today they call them Celebrations of Life. They start with a wake, have a sacred rite or service, and end with a gathering where a meal is served, or at least a table laden with finger food. We celebrate births, weddings, and baptisms with rites and parties, so why not gender transitioning from he to she?

When I asked Christopher what he thought of this idea, he said, "No funeral. I want a party. A riotous, drunken Irish-like party. A real celebration."

"Okay," I said, "but parties are the end of the celebration, after the sacred rite, just as wakes are the foreplay to the rite. I'd like a sacramental rite to bring closure to help me move on. Then we can have the party."

This rite, this formal saying goodbye to Christopher might have helped with my transition to accepting the loss of my relationship with a son. Raising and relating to a son is not the same as relating to a daughter. Having to switch your way of responding, reacting, and rearing a son is complex and confusing after thirty-two years of experience. You raise a boy not to cry, to play with trucks, to be a male. You raise a girl to play with dolls, to wear frilly pink dresses, to be a female. You are crafting, molding this small child into the expectations you have for them as an adult. Boyishness is rough and tumble, strong and stoic. Girlishness is soft and gentle, caring and compassionate.

I reared each one of my children in that respect. Holly was a princess at Halloween. Christopher was Darth Vader. Holly is feminine. Christopher is masculine. My adult daughter shares her feelings with me: her aspirations, her fears and joys. My adult son shares things with me: his job status, his latest hobby, what he fixed on his car, or what he barbequed for dinner last night. Never any feelings. Even today, he is not fully a female, because he often reacts and responds in the boyish manner in which he was raised. I will say, however, as of late he has begun to share some of his feelings.

A wake might have helped me let go of my expectations of a boyish Christopher or at least reset the internal pronoun from him to her just by talking with our friends about him at the wake. Wakes are those times when we talk about the deceased, dredge up old stories, cry a lot, laugh a lot, and revel in our memories to let them drift away into some thin space of time.

"He was always such a generous man," said his favorite cousin, the recipient of a loan.

"Christopher was so smart," said one of his college professors.

"He was a fabulous painter. I loved his pictures," said his art teacher.

"Did you know he smoked marijuana in school?" said his ninth-grade boarding school roommate.

"I'm going to miss him," said his best friend, Kevin.

In my mind's eye, I have often imagined how Christopher's Celebration of Life might look. It would not be in a church, of course. It could have been a private rite in our home. We have a large family room that would be ample. Thirty-two candles would grace the window sill of the bay window to represent his age at death. Lights would be dimmed to church-like reverence. Two urns of deep red roses, representing love and grief, would grace each side of the mantle. We would have Holy Communion to invite the presence of Jesus.

There would be eulogies from an assortment of friends. Even I would manage to give one, and perhaps even Christopher would share his thoughts on the loss of Christopher, the one being remembered, remembering himself. How unique. I can only leave that eulogy to my imagination. When I asked Christopher what he would say, he just stared at me and said, "I don't think I would have anything to say. I would just want to dance at the party to celebrate my being myself."

Touché. So, like her.

There would be music on my Steinway upright piano, probably being played by our church organist, a nice Christian woman who has known Christopher since childhood. She would not play the funereal kind, those dreadful dirges. No, this music would be contemporary and reflect Christopher's likes. I shudder to think of heavy rock or glam metal at this celebration.

Oh well, if that's what he wants, that's what he'll have. I don't know what those songs might be yet, as I didn't ask him.

There would be no body. The body was changed, not gone. Funny, at celebrations I've attended, it is said, "Life is not ended. It is only changed."

Not ended, changed. I must hold onto that thought. It will be my sanity anchor.

The pastor at the service would extol all his virtues: his Romanesque facial features, his bold and beautiful strokes of paint flung on a canvas, the laughter he evoked from others, his gentle presence as he danced at his prom, his love of nature. Only the good things, none of the bad. There would be no commendation of his soul into heaven as in a usual funeral service. There would be no committal of his body into the ground. The service would only be a remembrance of a young man who once lived, but was no more.

Although I've struggled many nights trying to understand gender dysphoria and many more nights letting go of a son who was now my daughter, I realized as I composed a eulogy in my head that the essence, the personality, the character of Christopher has not changed. He is still very much alive. Christopher is not dead. Not gone. A funeral, a Celebration of Life, won't solve anything or help me transition into accepting a she rather than a he. I'm not sure what will help. Perhaps just the tincture of time will be the healing balm. Maybe nothing. Maybe this dichotomy is just something I will always have sitting in my heart.

I keep a selection of special photos on the shelf behind my desk chair, mostly family photos to keep my loved ones close to me. One of them is of Christopher at about age eight. I swivel around, pick it up and run my hand over his face, remembering those long-ago times of raising a son.

Some days, I just want my beautiful baby boy back.

PRONOUNS AND NAMES

One of the most difficult transitions for family and friends was switching the pronoun. The son you have called "him," you must now call "her." It seems like such a tiny thing, but it is enormous. It has been over twelve years since her transition and the occasional "him" still slips out past our tongues to hang in the air until we fumble around for the "her" that should have first appeared.

For some of us, this transition was easier than for others. It was her stepfather, William, who mastered the pronoun first. He has only called her "him" twice that I recall. I was probably second. Others are still not there. New friends and neighbors have no difficulty, since they never knew Christopher. I called Christopher "him" for thirty-two years. To begin calling my "him" "her" was like trying to cough up a bone stuck in your throat. It wasn't necessarily painful physically, but it was difficult to get it out. There isn't a Heimlich maneuver to spit out the proper pronouns.

Years on end of accidentally spitting out the "he" instead of the "she" prompted me to say, "You know, my darling daughter, the pronoun problem will probably never go away entirely."

"It's okay, Mom. I know you're trying."

God bless her forgiving generosity. I'm now using the correct pronoun with her female gender about 99 percent of the time. Whenever I do slip, I have such a guilty feeling, but she is quick to say, "It's okay, Mom."

Along with the pronoun, we also struggled with the name change. Names are important. Names carry on family traditions. My brother is the third to carry on the paternal name. Many women, such as my stepdaughter-in-law, give their maiden names as middle names to their daughters. Several hundred years ago in some places, women's headstones bore maiden names with the notation, "Wife of …"

Many names have specific meanings, such as Maria for Christ's mother or Dolores for sadness. My sister had Downs Syndrome, so my mother named me Rita after Saint Rita, thinking she was the saint of the afflicted. She thought if I was named after that saint, I would protect my sister. Unfortunately, Saint Rita is the saint of impossible causes, but my mother never knew that. She was long dead when I found out. Some people don't like their birth names. I have a cousin named Maureen who was bullied about her name, often being called "Moron." She changed her name to Grace Marie after her grandmother. Names are important.

Although Christopher initially chose the name Wendy, in the end she legally changed her name to Kristen. I recall a conversation with her about various names she was considering. She went through all of her choices for first names: Wendy, Elizabeth, Emma, Nancy. What was ironic was I originally wanted to name my first daughter Emma, but no one else in the family liked it. They said it sounded like a name for a horse. Here, it was coming out of Christopher's mouth as one of her choices. Another name I always loved, but no one else in the family did, was Victoria. Christopher selected that as her new middle name. No one was more pleased than I. I actually wanted to call her Tori, but she nixed that. Eventually, she settled on Kristen for her first name.

Christopher selected the first name Kristen because she thought it would be easier for the family to transition from calling her Chris (her nickname) to calling her Kris. In retrospect, I think it might have been easier to adapt to any other name that disassociated us from "him" and "he." What has happened is we call her Kristen, not Kris, which I think helped us sort out the pronouns. On the other hand, just recently, Kristen, William, and I were getting a Dairy Queen. William was finding us a table and I was placing the order. I said to Kristen, "Will you ask William what she wants?" Some days you just can't win.

While I had never thought that she might want to change her last name, I was dead wrong. In the past Kristen, had a bumpy relationship with her father, bickering over one thing or another. This renaming seemed to her a chance to shed part of the connection to her father by choosing a different surname. She wanted to use my maiden name, Beauchamp. While I was flattered, I asked her to reconsider. I knew it would alienate her father forever, which would not be a good thing. People change and relationships change. If a relationship is cut off, there is little hope of reconciliation. I didn't want that for Kristen and her father. Ultimately, she agreed and kept her birth surname. Whew! That was one decision I wouldn't have to explain to her father, who was having his own difficulties with her gender dysphoria, pronouns, and the loss of his son, his male heir.

Whenever I talk to Kristen on those infrequent days when she wants to talk about serious life issues, I see the degree of turmoil and inner torment that she is enduring as a transgender person. Her quivering lip, eyes filling up, and the catch in her voice speak volumes. I hold her hand and give her a hug, choking back my own tears, silently praying that I can make her life perfect.

ALL IN THE FAMILY

For most of the year 2000, the knowledge of Kristen's gender dysphoria was something shared only by our small family. By the end of the year, however, it was time for us to come out as well. You can only call your son, "her" to her face and "him" to the rest of the world for so long without slipping up. I have finally gotten to the point where I think of her as a girl when I tell stories of Kristen's childhood, so it now becomes harder to call "her" "him."

Each year at Christmas, we send out one of those either beloved or hated Christmas letters, depending on whom you ask. Personally, I love to get them and catch up on the news of the past year from friends we don't see often enough. As we contemplated our 2000 letter, we decided that it was time to let our circle of friends and family in on the secret. Well, almost.

"Kristen, we are putting our annual letter together. How do you feel about us letting folks know about your gender change?"

"Uh, I don't know. Can I think about it and get back to you?" she asked with an audible pause in her voice.

My shoulders slumped. I wanted an answer now.

"Okay, but can you get back to me soon?"

"Sure, Mom. But are you sure this is okay with you? I mean, what will your clergy friends think? What will your congregation or your bishop think?"

"I'm not sure, but I'm ready to tell our friends and the family so I don't feel like I'm always hiding something so important."

Her comments however, made me realize that I wasn't ready to let those in my clerical life in on this aspect of my life. Since Kristen didn't attend my church or even live in the same state, no one in that part of my life had to know. Yet. Yes, there would be exceptions, so our list that year would be two letters, one with the secret, one without. I wasn't ready to totally reveal this part of my life to all.

After some days, Kristen called back.

"Hi, mom. I've thought about the letter. I'm ready to let you put my gender in it."

"Oh, Kristen, thanks. I've thought about our last conversation, and you helped me realize there are some people who don't have to know."

"Yeah, I thought so."

"Well, I've decided my church and clergy people don't need to know. I'm not afraid of their reaction, I don't think. But since they might never meet you, I don't see any reason to tell them, at least not now."

I closed my eyes and held my breath, waiting for her response. Would it offend her?

"That's okay with me. I'd rather you didn't tell them anyway. What about William's family? Are you going to tell them?"

"I'm not sure. I should leave it up to him. Since he hasn't seen his son in many years, I doubt he will want him to know." And as it turned out, that was another person who would not know. Yet.

"You know, Mom, not everyone is going to understand my being a tranny." That label caught me by surprise as my head jerked back in surprise.

"Tranny?"

"Yes, Mom, that's what we are sometimes called."

Something else I had to learn was the transgender terminology. I didn't like the term but acknowledged it as part of that genre of people.

"Mom, you know some people won't understand or accept me as a female. Are you ready to be rejected because of me?"

Wow, talk about a perceptive child.

Taking a deep breath and swallowing hard, I said, "Yes, I have thought about this for almost a year, and I know some people will walk this walk with us, and others will not. I'm prepared for the rejection of those who don't, but there won't be many of them. Our friends are solid Christians, and I'm counting on their love."

I hope.

And so it came to pass that we wrote two letters: one with the news, one without. In one short paragraph, we told sixty-some recipients that our son, Christopher, was now our daughter, Kristen. Today, we send most of these letters by email. In 2000, they were all sent by snail mail. As I sat at our dining room table, Christmas carols playing softly, the tree lighted and festooned with decorations, I signed and folded each letter, put the label on the envelope, and slipped the letter inside.

Once again, I thought about the possibility of rejection from this person or that person. A wave of fear gnawed at my stomach with each lick of the stamp. Others, I knew, would understand. Still, I worried this news would be met with great reluctance to support us. I put the ones I worried about in a separate pile so I could rethink them one last time. I pulled one to a business friend overseas, not ready for him to know, addressed a new envelope and slipped in the "without" letter. William's family also received the "without" letter, as did all my clerical friends. There would be time for them later.

I put my packet of letters in a brown paper bag and took our family secret for their ride to be delivered. The last growl of fear punched me in the gut as the envelopes slipped into the dark recesses of the outgoing mail slot at the post office. No turning back now. It was out there. Bring it on. I had an unexpected sense of relief as I walked out of the post office into the winter sunshine. No more secrets. Almost.

One day passed. Nothing. Two days passed. No word from anyone.

On the third day, I thought, *Oh God, everyone must have the letter by now. They must all hate us.*

I sat and cried in the corner of the couch, wondering how people could be so cruel.

It was going to be a dismal Christmas, I thought, as I blew my nose and soaked up another box of tissues.

Well, if that's what it's going to be like, so be it. God will just have to get us all through this. Right, God?

It was on the fifth day we received a call from a cousin from Michigan. Oh great, he was the ultra-conservative one.

Here comes the first condemnation.

What I heard on the other end was, "We want you to know that we love you and we love Kristen. You have our complete support, and please let us know if there is anything we can do for you."

I could barely speak as a torrent of tears blurred my vision and closed my throat.

"Wow. Thanks," I croaked. "You have no idea how much

that means to me."

Then I just broke down sobbing and handed the phone to William. I couldn't speak, but a big smile washed over my face. If the most conservative in my family accepted Kristen, maybe it wouldn't be so bad after all.

Over the next few days, we were flooded with telephone calls from people we hadn't spoken to in years. Those that we didn't hear from were the ones we knew were probably having some trouble with it. And why not? When we first learned of transgender dysphoria, it was confusing for us. Even today, the scientific community doesn't understand why or how this happens to one person and not another. It's a new phenomenon in the continuum that makes up human beings.

There are many people who know about Kristen and to this day have never brought up the subject. It is as if Christopher/Kristen fell off the face of the earth, never to reappear. Sad but true, and it did hurt our feelings, since we considered them close enough to share this dramatic change in our life. Concluding it is their issue, not ours, has helped us accept this silent rejection. When we see them, which is rarely, it isn't a subject we discuss. Of course, if Kristen happens to be with us, the elephant is in the room. We see it in their eyes, and we hear it in their strained conversation.

Surprisingly, some of the people we felt might have a problem with it, our conservative friends, have been our biggest supporters, a support system for us where we are able to talk to about it openly. Honestly, I'm not sure what I expected when those letters hit the mail slot. What I learned was that many of our family and friends were curious and open, asking us questions about what it meant to be transgender. I could only answer from my limited understanding and refer them to the book, *True Selves.* Conversations often went like this:

"I've never heard of this. How do you get that way?"

"As I understand it, one is born that way. Kristen says she knew about it since she was four or five."

"If you ever need us, we're here for you. We know this must be a difficult time for you."

Or, "Is there a cure for this?"

"Uh, no. It is like being born with blue eyes or black hair. It's like being a homosexual or lesbian."

"But how does it happen?

"We don't know. Some say it is a hormone wash at five-weeks' development, but no one really knows for sure."

"We love all of you no matter what and will love Christopher just the same."

And on and on. Seeking understanding, giving unconditional love. Our letter opened our world of friends and family to the reality of Kristen being transgender. As we found out, this was the beginning of life with a transgender person. For her, and for us. It was a journey none of us imagined when that letter went out.

A WORLD UNRAVELED...

In mid-January of 2001, as I was settling into my new ministry at The Church of the Resurrection several months after we moved to Delaware, Kristen's world began to unravel. We had no idea how unraveled it would become. Annie's MS was getting worse, Kristen had quit a rather good job as manager of a photography store, and she and Annie suffered serious emotional and financial problems. It had been two years since Annie's diagnosis and Kristen was her primary caregiver. Annie's MS was a progressive form, and she was almost completely confined to her motorized wheelchair within a few months.

For Annie, her wheelchair became her prison and her days of smiling and days of weeping vacillated from bearable to unbearable. As a consequence of these wild mood swings, it was becoming more and more difficult for Kristen to move Annie, bathe her, feed her, and respond appropriately to her moods. Annie, always the independent, take-charge person, frustrated by her medical limitations, would fling verbal abuse and orders at Kristen, demanding more from her than she could emotionally handle. It was this stress-inducing situation at home that precipitated Kristen quitting her job, which in turn put a huge financial burden on them. Our regular phone calls were stressful for all of us.

"Mom, can you send me some money to pay our rent and buy some food?"

"Sure. Have you found another job yet?"

"No, Mom. Please. I'm too busy taking care of Annie. She had another bad episode this week, and I had to get her to the hospital. I can't leave her alone."

"Oh no. I'm sorry, I didn't know. How are you holding up?"

"Mom, I don't know how much longer I can do this. Can you please help me?"

"We'll be right there."

The dogwood tree outside my window was just beginning to leaf. I always love this time of year with the birth of budding green trees mingled with the burst of flowers offering up a kaleidoscope of color. I called my Senior Warden at church and explained that I had a family emergency and needed to be away for a few days and would be back by Saturday. The daffodils outside my front porch always signaled a time of hope and renewal for me. As I packed our large green suitcase, I wondered what hope there was for Annie and Kristen. It was William who broke my somber silence.

"What do you think we will find when we arrive?" asked William.

"I don't know." I replied, holding up two tops I was packing, trying to decide which one to bring, wishing I had an answer to his question.

"What should we do?" he pressed on, stacking his underwear in a corner of the suitcase.

Always the practical one, I said, "The first thing we must do is get some food in the house, I would imagine. Then I guess we'll have to sit down and talk to them. See what they need."

As I climbed into bed, I felt an icy blanket of fear gripping my heart. Fear of the unknown. Unknown because I had no answer to their dilemma. I am a planner, I like to know what to do in any given situation, but I didn't know what to do this night. I tossed first on my right side, then on my left side, repeating that restless dance until the dawn woke me up.

Just as the dawn crested through the pine trees, we loaded the van in the pouring rain and took off on a rescue journey without a clue as to what we would do. The spring colors were muted behind the gray curtain of rain. As we continued north, the maple and oak trees grew barer and barer. Our conversation on this 600-mile plus journey was mostly conjecture about how to help Annie and Kristen.

"Do you think Annie should be put in some kind of assisted

living?' I asked

"Maybe, but maybe we could arrange for some type of in-home care," responded William.

"What about Kristen? What will happen to her?" I shot back. "We can't afford to support her, and I doubt her father can either. Or even half for that matter. Well, we at least know the present situation is not tenable, either emotionally or financially."

William gripped the steering wheel tighter and muttered, "I know, but I don't have the answers right now. I'll call Tom when we get there and see if he has any ideas."

I sighed in despair of ever finding a good outcome. William the pragmatist suggested we take a wait and see approach.

"Maybe Kristen and Annie will have some thoughts on this. After all, it is their life we are talking about. I don't think we can barge in there and order them around."

I retreated into my safe place of silence to ponder his last suggestion. As the miles flew by, we broke the silence from time to time to offer one solution after another. I think we analyzed every possible scenario from doing nothing to doing everything. From time to time, we talked about other thing: What was happening in the church, how did we like our new home, small, petty, mundane things. We are not ones to dwell incessantly on impossible-to-deal-with subjects. We'd figure that out later. I kept shaking my shoulders as if it would make everything better, or make the perfect solution magically appear.

Arriving in town, I spotted a Safeway supermarket and William did a quick U-turn into the parking lot.

"I don't know what they need, but we can get some of the basics."

"Should we go to the motel first?" William suggested as he pulled into a handy parking spot near the entrance.

"No, I want to see what's ahead of us first. Then we can check in."

It took us longer than usual to find the food in an unfamiliar store. The bread was on the right, not the left, the dairy was in the back, not the front, the produce was in the middle, not the side. After what seemed like forever, we bought what we considered enough food for a week. The staples: bread, butter, milk, eggs, lunch meat, hamburger, chicken thighs, cereal, vegetables, rice. Basic stuff.

Parking in front of the small yellow cottage they rented, we left our booty in the van and walked up to the front door. The house had a small porch across the front with a barbeque grill nestled in the corner along with a ratty, well-worn, forlorn wooden rocker missing only Whistler's Mother. There was no doorbell, so we knocked. Kristen answered and we walked into a house in total disarray.

The living room was sparsely furnished with only a sofa, a

side table, a lamp, a bed, and a television. Books, magazines, a vacuum, newspapers, a couple of bath towels, and several full ashtrays also populated this room. The sofa was old, swayback, with cushions that had cups in the middle from years of use. The layer of dust must have been there for months. The shades were drawn and there was little light, only what emanated from the TV. Annie was in her wheelchair posted in front of the TV where she apparently spent her days.

Kristen had set up her desk, computer, and filing cabinets in what was the dining room, surrounded by stacks and stacks of papers, files, and books. It was like a command center with monitors and keyboards surrounding her desk chair.

It was the kitchen, however, that snapped me right back to 1988 and the kitchen in the apartment she had shared with her first wife, Mariah. There were dirty dishes everywhere, including in the microwave and oven. You couldn't see the counters or the stovetop, which were piled high with more dirty dishes, empty pizza boxes, filthy rags, and unidentifiable clumps of long dead food. The refrigerator was empty except for a few eggs and a quart of milk on the edge of sour. Everything was filthy and it was evident that it hadn't been cleaned in months and months. I could feel the nausea rising in my gut. We put the food in the empty refrigerator and cupboards, then went into the living room to begin sorting out what had to be done.

They had no money, no medical insurance, and no income. Kristen was exhausted after two stressful caregiving years. There were dark circles under her eyes. She obviously hadn't eaten lately, as her clothes hung limply on her frame. Annie locked her eyes on the TV, barely acknowledging our presence. We later learned that her mind was deteriorating from her MS and she was often confused. This could have been one of those times.

We began the arduous process of getting Annie on Medicaid and food stamps. Kristen had already gone through the long, drawn-out process of getting Annie on Social Security disability, but they were still awaiting the first payment. Knowing that Kristen could not be trusted with cash, we bought food coupons from a local grocery store and gave them to Kristen to buy food for several weeks. All in all, we made several more trips to Connecticut. Each trip brought us to the realization that there was much, much more going on than we were told.

To get Annie on Medicaid, we learned from a case worker she and Kristen would have to get a divorce. It was an uneasy decision, but one that had to be made. Both objected, neither one wanting to end their marriage, but both also being stretched to the point of having nowhere else to turn. Annie needed medical help that would only be available if she had Medicaid. At this point in the progression of her disease, Annie really had no choice as her care was physically and financially beyond Kristen.

William and I couldn't support them, but we all understood something had to be done. Kristen found a local lawyer, and once more I found myself paying for her divorce. The divorce was final in June, and Annie began receiving Medicaid and food stamps. I was much relieved that some progress was being in made in stabilizing their life together.

During one of our trips, Annie said to me, "I want to move back to Shelton to be near my family. I want to go to the place where my mother stayed."

While her voice was slurred as the disease grew worse, she was able to understand Kristen could no longer take care of her physical needs. There was a nice assisted living place in Shelton that we contacted. Mercifully, they had room for her.

Once her monthly Social Security checks began in July, we began making the arrangements for Annie to move. We all knew she needed professional assistance, but this decision was more difficult than the decision to get a divorce. I sensed that Annie knew her relationship with Kristen was literally ending. We knew it too. No one was happy about this outcome, the end of a marriage, the end of a relationship, but then no one knew Annie's health would deteriorate so much and so quickly. It was Kristen who was the most upset.

"Mom, I promised Annie I would never put her in a nursing home. I can't do this," she said, tears staining her cheeks.

"Honey, I know what you promised Annie, but you know you can't take care of her. She needs more help than you are able to give her."

"I know, I know, but I promised, Mom," she managed to choke out between sobs.

I could see the guilt settle in her eyes and knew this move would pierce her heart. I also felt that it would be liberating for both. I sensed it would free Kristen to be Kristen. I sensed it would free Annie to get appropriate medical care. By the end of July, Kristen moved Annie into a cottage at the same assisted living facility where Annie's mother had spent her last days.

Kristen was then left alone in the house in Connecticut and had full access to the checking account that contained Annie's SSI checks. As the leaves began to fall on the crape myrtle tree, we found out Kristen was not paying Annie's bills when the manager of the assisted living facility called me and said we owed $1,100 in room rent. "What?" I asked, "Have you called Kristen?"

"Yes, she keeps promising to send the money, but it isn't in the mail. You were listed as an alternative contact, so we called you."

"Thank you. I'll take care of this."

I slammed down the phone, banged my fist on the desk, let out a stress releasing primal scream, and called Kristen.

"Why haven't you paid Annie's bills?"

"I don't have the money anymore."

"Why not, for God's sake?"

"Well, I just seem to spend it on other things."

"There is nothing more important than paying Annie's bills and your rent," I yelled.

I hung up. We paid her overdue room rent while Annie managed, with the help of the staff, to get the joint checking account closed and her disability checks sent directly to her. Closing the checking account severed the last material link they had to each other. It would be the last time I had any contact with Annie or anyone else regarding her care.

Kristen rarely visited Annie after her move to assisted living, but I understand they did talk frequently on the phone. The guilt of putting Annie in what was considered a nursing home was simply too much for Kristen to bear. Each face-to-face visit became a stark reminder of what seemed to her a betrayal of Annie, and Kristen told me how Annie always took great pains to remind her of that broken promise.

On a visit to see Annie some nine years ago, Kristen wanted to take her out to dinner as a special treat. The staff put her in a collapsible wheel chair and Kristen wheeled her out to her car. The car was a two-door sporty Acura Integra which sits low to the ground. Kristen maneuvered the chair alongside the passenger door of the car, opened the door, and moved the chair as close as possible. As she was lifting Annie from the wheelchair into the car Annie's foot got caught in the foot-prop of the wheelchair, shifting her weight off-balance. Kristen felt her grip on Annie loosen and before she knew it, Annie was on the ground in the small space between her wheelchair and the car. Her dress was hitched up near her waist, and her left elbow was scraped and bleeding. Annie's breathing was labored and Kristen called for medical assistance to get her back to her room. Her plans for a nice dinner and evening out were ruined. She returned home, never to see Annie face-to-face again.

On May 23, 2012, my birthday, Annie died in the nursing home where she had been confined for the past eleven years. Strangely enough, it wasn't her MS that took her life, but stomach cancer. To this day, through our many discussions about Annie, Kristen carries her guilt around in her heart. But at least she knows that Annie's wish to be buried next to her mother was granted. I was never close to Annie, so my grief was shallow. But her death at age fifty-eight was still a shock. MS isn't a death sentence, so I expected to her to live much longer. I have never asked her, but I believe Annie's death also put some of Kristen's guilt to rest as well.

In late August, Kristen's father helped her move out of Connecticut and in with some friends in Newport, Rhode Island. By this time, Kristen had obtained all the certification she needed for her gender reassignment surgery and had changed her name on all of her records except her birth certificate. Until recently, most birth certificates cannot be changed until after reassignment surgery. Within a month, Kristen found a job in a photography store and finally had a steady income. She was even making some additional money photographing weddings, and I kept reminding her to save some money for her surgery. However, while she intended to save these funds, her living expenses such as her car, her rent, her cigarettes, always took precedence. There was never anything saved.

In January of 2002, her friends in Newport told her their daughter was coming to live with them and Kristen had to leave. For the first time in her thirty-four years, Kristen would be living alone. She found a small apartment in Providence, and we bought her a double bed, which was all that would fit in the ten by twelve foot, third floor walkup. We shipped her some household items and linens, and she was on her own. I often wondered how being alone would be for her. She never complained about her living arrangement, although once she said, "I'm kind of lonely."

My heart twisted with a remembered pain of some long-ago loneliness I had experienced.

"Oh, I'm so sorry to hear that."

It was a lame comment, but it was all I could muster. I knew I couldn't be a magic genie and rustle up a companion or room-mate for her. Maybe she would adjust.

Although she was employed, she could barely afford the $660 a month rent. So, both her father and I subsidized her with extra money here, extra money there. We were sure it would all work out for her. At least that was our hope for her and for us.

Then in March she lost her job.

GOOD INTENTIONS

Within a few weeks, Kristen found a job at another photography store closer to her apartment. We breathed a bit easier and our wallets rejoiced. We spoke on the phone weekly. She seemed settled in and content at work. She was working as a portrait photographer, and she would regale us with stories of her encounters with fussy clients. One story sticks in my mind of a portrait of a dog she was doing for a magazine cover. The client was so particular she kept complaining that a single hair on the dog's tail didn't look right. After twenty or so revisions, Kristen told them to take their dog and move to another planet.

I'm not sure the picture ever did end up on a cover, although she did have three other dog portraits featured on dog magazine covers. Weddings were anathema to her. She would gripe about how almost everyone was drunk and it was always difficult to capture just the right moments. Our conversations were usually upbeat, except for those rare times when our call interrupted an episode of loneliness she was going through. I was beginning to hope this would be the end of any more drama. Hah. Somehow, to paraphrase an old cliché, hope springs eternal in a mother's breast.

In July of that year, she called and told us she had found a roommate. Of course, I grilled her about all the particulars of meeting this girl: where she came from, where she worked, her education, parents, friends, likes, dislikes, etc. While I was rather curious how two people would be able to live in her small apartment, I didn't ask. Turns out her new roommate was also a male to female transgender girl named Beverly who would be sharing the rent. Well, at least she had some income.

Kristen met her at the Fantasia Fair in Provincetown on Cape Cod. The Fantasia Fair is a week-long celebration of gender diversity and the longest running annual conference in the transgender world. I would have rather heard her say she met her in church, but then neither of my children are regular church-goers. God-fearing, yes, church-going, no.

Without even knowing this girl, I felt uneasy about the situation. But it seemed as if they both had good intentions. I kept telling myself how supportive it would be for Kristen to have another transgender person to share the ups and downs of transitioning. As supportive as her family wanted to be, we could hardly relate to this transition in any meaningful way, except maybe to continue to say, "We love you." Still, my gut told me this was not a good situation. Don't ask me for some deeper meaning, because there wasn't one. Eventually, my intuition was validated.

We had acquired a Maltese puppy from a breeder in Massachusetts and were planning to pick him up in early August. I called Kristen and asked if we might stop in Providence and take them out to dinner. I said we could meet Beverly and see their apartment. She agreed. I hadn't seen Kristen in over a year and was anxious to see her, meet her new roommate, and see her apartment.

I honestly don't remember much of the trip up there. What I do recall is I spent much of the time looking out the window as the billboards flew by like giant flashcards. While the day was bright and clear for our trip, my mind was muddied with uncertainties about what we would find when we arrived in Providence. Questions danced in my head: What would she look like, would she "pass" easily as a woman, would she have a sparkling personality, would we like her?

"I hope this roommate works out," I said, as we drove on the almost deserted, boring interstate.

"Me too," replied William, "Me too. It'll be good for Kristen to have someone living with her. She's been so lonely living alone."

"Yes, I agree. I just hope it works out. I so want this Beverly person to be nice."

I guess I really meant acceptable to me. Mothers are so fussy.

"I'm looking forward to seeing how they're managing in her small apartment."

We arrived at her place around 4:00 p.m. and knocked on her door, breathless from the three-story climb. Kristen opened the door, hugs all around as she ushered us in. The door opened into the largest room, about the size of my ten-foot square office cubicle. The only piece of furniture in it was the double bed in front of a double window and covered by a printed quilt. Some books were stacked in one corner. To the left was a small galley kitchen, and to the right was a full bathroom, from which Beverly appeared to greet us.

The apartment was inordinately neat for Kristen's unkempt style, and I commented, "Everything looks so neat."

Beverly said, "It was a mess, but we cleaned it up when we knew you were coming."

My organized, neat-freak mind thought,

Thank God. Maybe Beverly will keep the place presentable. Presentable for me that is, as I doubt they will be entertaining much in this little garret.

With no place to sit and visit, we made a hasty exit to a local Olive Garden.

Dinner was uneventful, pleasant, fact-gathering. Each one of us, in our own way, were putting on our happy faces. Smiles all around, pleasantries exchanged. I, of course, was the designated grill person.

"So where is your hometown, Beverly?"

"What do you do to earn a living?"

"Where did you go to school?"

"Have you lived in Providence long?"

"How long since you transitioned?

I've never been one to hesitate going right to the point or asking the difficult and very personal questions.

Here's what I remember I learned at that meal. Beverly was injured on a construction job several years ago and was on substantial disability. She also had some other independent income, because she was footing the entire expenses for the both of them. We learned Kristen no longer had a job, but she would be looking for one. Good intentions. Beverly had transitioned about a year earlier and had brow shaving, cheek implants, and breast enhancement surgery. She was still pre-surgical genitally. She was tall, lean, with shimmering red hair, and stunning. Kristen too was tall, lean, with wheaten blond hair, and also stunning. They were radiant this evening. I liked Beverly. I relaxed a bit, and my earlier fears subsided a bit but didn't completely go away.

We invited Kristen to accompany us up to Massachusetts to

collect our puppy, so we had an opportunity to visit, get acquainted with the puppy, let Kristen hold him, have lunch together, nice family stuff. There wasn't a hint the entire day of anything out of the ordinary, anything askew, anything foreboding.

William was going to celebrate his seventieth turn around the sun this year. As a way to celebrate, I made reservations at one of our favorite Inns near Providence and invited his entire family for dinner with us the day after Thanksgiving. It was to be a surprise for William. All he knew was we were going to stay at the inn for some R & R through the weekend. He loved inn weekends, and we looked forward to enjoying ourselves.

Kristen had been invited to join us for William's birthday dinner the day after Thanksgiving. She accepted. The day of the dinner as I was getting dressed, my cell phone rang. It was Kristen saying she wasn't feeling well and couldn't make the dinner. I was let down, but had learned not to protest since it rarely accomplished anything positive. An hour later, she called again.

"Mom, do you think I should come anyway?"

"No dear, you should take care of yourself."

"You won't be mad at me?"

"Of course not. If you are sick, take care."

"Okay, but I feel bad."

"Well don't. It's okay."

For the next two hours, she kept calling me every half-hour, asking me whether she should join us. The last call came just as we were entering the dining room of the inn with the rest of the family. Again, I told her to stay home and rest. I turned off my phone and took my seat with the others. My worry meter was working overtime, and I was completely puzzled by these pleas for assurance. It just wasn't like Kristen, but I couldn't sort out why. What I didn't know then, but did much later, was that she was high on cocaine and literally out of her mind. More about that later.

One week later, we were back in Providence. Kristen had called about 10:00 a.m. the day before, sobbing, screaming, and yelling that she and Beverly had a huge argument about something I can't even remember, and she had taken a whole bottle of pills and was going to kill herself. I don't remember the details of the phone call, but a blanket of fear washed over me, and my legs went limp, as I closed my eyes to say a silent prayer.

Please God, let her be all right. Please.

I told her I would get help and call her back. Then my organized mind kicked into high gear. I had to save her. I had to. I wasn't sure exactly what had happened to precipitate this turn of events, but I knew I had to act now and find out later. Hands shaking, heart racing, I called her father who was about an hour and a half away and begged him to get over to her place. He agreed. Then I called 911, and they put me through to an ambulance company in Providence. I called Kristen back and told her an ambulance was on the way and so were we.

"No, Mom. I'm not getting in the ambulance."

"Yes, you are," I yelled with the fury of a frantic mother. "And, if you don't, your father is on the way and he will drive you to the hospital when he gets there if you are still alive."

This whole scenario was surreal, moving almost in slow motion, because I was actually holding my breath as I dashed around making those phone calls, throwing some clothes in a bag, calling William to come home from his part-time job in a local liquor store. I was moving as fast as I could in a whirlpool of alarm for the life of my child.

Amidst great protest, Kristen was taken to the hospital and it was there some six hours later that we found her in the hall on a gurney, her father sitting in the waiting room, head in hands, not seeing us until I tapped him on the shoulder. He looked old and drawn, haggard. We went in to see Kristen who kept insisting that nothing was wrong, that she was fine. I wasn't buying it. Tom, William, and the doctor weren't buying it either. After determining that she hadn't done her body any serious harm, she was transferred to a psychiatric hospital for evaluation.

Kristen was terrified of being put in an unsafe environment, so it was at this point we let the doctor know she was a pre-surgical transgender so she would not be put in with men, but would have appropriate accommodations. This issue of accommodations is always a concern since, pre-surgical transgender people cannot be housed in gender specific jails, hospitals, or detention centers. In today's atmosphere of openness around the transgender population, there is a lot of political discussion, some good, some not so good. For example, some states have already passed laws indicating what bathroom facility they must use. Discrimination against transgender people is widespread, but acceptance is coming only slowly.

While Kristen was in the psychiatric ward, we visited the new apartment she and Beverly had rented in September. It was a large, three-bedroom apartment in what Beverly described as a drug-riddled neighborhood, unlike the safe neighborhood they had left. It was trashed. There was hardly a square foot of floor that was not covered with boxes, clothing, computer parts, dishes, and other assorted items. There were dirty dishes, pots, pans, and remnants of food on counters, chairs, tables, and the floor. Ashtrays were overflowing everywhere, as were empty liquor bottles. The smell was intolerable, and it was difficult even to consider staying for more than a few minutes.

Beverly then showed us bullet holes in the wall of one bedroom. Apparently, during an argument, Kristen had threatened Beverly with a gun she had acquired somewhere. In the heat of the argument, she had discharged it into the wall. Tom confiscated the gun and later stored it in a safe place at his home where she would not have access to it. It was at this point that I began to realize I had no idea of the enormity of Kristen's situation. Guns, alcohol, drug neighborhood? I didn't like what I saw, heard, or what I even dared to think about the life this child of mine was living.

Two days later Tom, Alicia, Beverly, myself, and William sat in the visitor's conference room of the psychiatric facility. It was about twelve feet by twenty feet, with soft padded chairs lining the walls like sentinels watching an imaginary play in the open central portion of the room. We all chose our seats and waited. I kept picking at my nails, contemplating the next step, ignoring the others in the room. We were waiting to talk to the doctor in charge. Tom and William sat together chatting, while Alicia was quietly praying, occasionally wiping a tear from her eyes. Beverly sat off by herself, making no effort to engage in conversation with any of us.

It wasn't long before Kristen and the doctor entered the arena. As the doctor scanned the room, he had a surprised look on his face, which I thought a bit odd. However, he began the conversation by saying that in all his years at this psychiatric facility, he had never seen such a large support group of family show up for a meeting. We all looked around at each other and smiled weakly, saying nothing. I moved over to sit next to William and took his hand. Kristen sat next to me. She looked tired, worried. She took my hand. Tom and Alicia sat nearby with Beverly.

The doctor, a tall, slightly balding, lean man in the mandatory white jacket, told us after his examination during the last two days, he didn't believe Kristen was in any danger of hurting herself in the future. He said he was ready to discharge her and asked us where she would be living. During these past few days, we had stayed with Tom and Alicia and spent many hours discussing the path forward. For over ten years, both her father and I had provided financial support in one form or another to Kristen. Tom and I were now drained financially as well as emotionally.

We were at a loss as to what to do for our daughter and perhaps more at a loss as to exactly what it was that constituted this child of ours. The two stepparents, William and Alicia, joined in our frustration and concern. We all knew that Kristen needed a lot of help, and continuing to simply throw money at her would not solve anything. Before our meeting, the four of us had agreed that Kristen should come live with us in Delaware, where we could get her medical and psychological help.

When the doctor asked where Kristen would be living, I said, "She should come home with us."

Beverly jumped in quickly and said, "She'll come home with

me."

The doctor then asked Kristen her choice. There was a long pause, many exchanges of looks between us and Beverly before she finally said, "I'll go home with Beverly."

I was so let down. I turned to Kristen, held both of her hands, looked her directly in the eyes and said, "Kristen, we can't help you unless you come home with us."

She put her head down and didn't answer. She didn't change her mind. My gut said this was not a good thing, but she was an adult and able to make her own decisions. I was helpless. We thanked the doctor, collected our coats, hugged each other, said our goodbyes, and silently left the room to go our separate ways.

A few weeks later, Kristen called to tell us she lost her job again but was certain she would find another one soon. Meanwhile, Beverly was supporting them.

Good intentions.

Much, much later we learned, to our utter horror, both Beverly and Kristen were wrapped in the arms of an expensive cocaine habit. Drugs drove Kristen back to Beverly and back on the road to hell. Although Beverly had a decent income, support of this kind of habit was getting beyond her ability to pay for it. She and Kristen were in the process of developing a pornographic website whereby they would be advertising themselves as transgender prostitutes. Those seeking aberrant sexual pleasures were apparently willing to pay large amounts of money to have sex with people who appeared to be half-man, half-woman.

I had known about Kristen's occasional use of marijuana and LSD while in boarding school over the years but would never have suspected it had reached such huge proportions. Personally, I'm not sure I would have wanted to know about it at the time. There are some things the parent of an adult simply doesn't need to know. But I am certain that I would not so easily have surrendered my daughter to go back to the apartment in Providence with Beverly had I known.

It was New Year's Day of 2002, about 8:00 a.m., and I was just coming out of the shower when the phone rang. William was downstairs getting my coffee as we prepared to spend the day watching all the football games. I grabbed a towel and ran into the bedroom to answer the phone.

"Rita?"

"Yes."

"This is Beverly."

Odd. Why would she be calling me?

"Hi, Beverly. What's up?" I managed as I wrapped the towel around my bust.

"Kristen and I went to a party last night, and Kristen left with a man."

Okay, this was weird. Now what? I could feel the sick feeling something was dreadfully wrong creeping all around my skin.

"And?" I asked.

"She hasn't come home."

"Is this unusual?"

"Yes. I thought perhaps Kristen had come down to your place."

"No, she hasn't. But please let me know when she does come home."

I hung up, threw on a robe, and headed downstairs to talk to William. Fear of some awful thing like a kidnapping, a runaway, or even a murder paralyzed my thinking. I sat on the sofa in our family room, turned on our gas fireplace, sipped my coffee, and just let my brain flip through all the possible reasons Kristen didn't go home with Beverly. Maybe I shouldn't even worry. It was New Year's Eve, people get drunk, and people do silly things. Perhaps she went home with this guy and would be home soon.

As time went by and Kristen didn't come home, I was frantic as fear dug its gnarly fingernails deeper into my soul. For the rest of the day and night, Beverly and I called each other regularly to check in. The calls were short.

"Home yet?"

"No,"

"Okay. Talk to you later."

At 10:00 p.m., I told her that if Kristen wasn't home by 9:00 a.m. the next morning, I was filing a missing person report with the Providence police. Someone in Kristen's condition (a female outwardly with male equipment) could easily be murdered. If the wrong person had perhaps tried to assault her or given her the date-rape drug and then found out this woman was actually a man, it could have disastrous results: a beating, maiming, or even death. We worried and prayed.

Neither William nor I got much sleep that night, holding each other, assuring each other that it would all be fine, trying to be positive. I was sitting in our bedroom reading alcove by 6:00 a.m., watching the clock, waiting for either a phone call or to make a phone call myself. I decided it was best to get dressed in case I had to leave quickly. I showered and dressed. By 7:30 a.m., I was in our great room sipping my morning coffee and watching the dancing flames of the fireplace. At 8:30 a.m., Beverly called to say that Kristen was home.

"Oh, thank God. Thank God. Is she all right? Let me talk to her?"

"Hi, Mom."

My first impulse was to scream, "Where have you been? We've been worried sick."

Instead, I said, "Are you okay?"

"Yeah, Mom. I'm fine. I was with a friend and my cell phone battery was dead."

Well, sure. That explains everything. But it was still two days of sheer hell for us.

"Well, I'm glad you're home and safe," I managed so say in as a calm a manner as possible.

"I'll call you tomorrow, Mom. I'm tired now."

Good intentions.

Two hours later the pavement of good intentions buckled.

COMING HOME

With the early morning call on January second letting us know Kristen was home, we relaxed and went about our life. But at 10:30 a.m., as we were driving home from a trip to the bank, another phone call came that would change our lives for an undefined future, though at the time we didn't understand how. Kristen was sobbing, screaming, and yelling that Beverly was beating her up and the police were there. I asked to speak to the police, since my usually articulate daughter was incoherent. The police assured me that it was a minor domestic violence call and was now completely under control. I again spoke to Kristen and asked her if she wanted to come home. Again, no, with a reassurance that everything would be just fine.

I hung up, mystified by the fact my hysterical daughter had called, obviously for some reason. Help? Support? What? It was so confusing.

As we turned into our driveway, I said, "I'll call later this afternoon just to see how she is managing. Something dreadful is going on in that house."

A mother's fear for her child is always lurking in the back of her heart, but for me, at this moment, that fear was front and center.

Once back home, I went into the great room, grabbed a cup of coffee, and headed for my office downstairs. Twenty minutes later, my cellular phone rang again and Kristen was screaming about her scalp being twisted off and pinched by Beverly, with blood all over.

Oh, my God. This is serious.

She wept about being punched and thrown against the wall. With deep breathless sobs, she said she was being killed by Beverly. I asked if the police had been called. Yes. Where was Beverly now? Locked in a closet. Could you get out of the house? Yes. Then go and drive to your father's house. It was the best advice I could think of at the moment.

That's not exactly what happened, but Kristen got out of harm's way. The police arrived shortly after I hung up with Kristen, and Beverly was taken from the locked closet and committed to Butler Psychiatric Hospital for thirty day drug rehabilitation. Within the hour, Kristen's father arrived, as well as the owner of the apartment who had been called by the police. Tom called us and assured us that Kristen was not badly injured, which was a huge relief. Although it was only late morning, I really wanted a glass of wine instead of coffee. We talked about what next and Tom said Kristen could pay for half a month's rent. The owner, feeling sympathy for her, granted her the other half gratis, with the understanding that she would move out as soon as possible.

Tom said "She can come stay with me until we figure out some other arrangement."

Fortunately for us, we didn't have to make another emergency trip up to Providence, which was a huge relief since my job as full-time rector of my church needed my attention, and William was working part-time as a wine consultant at a nearby retail store.

During the next week, Kristen began the arduous task of moving out of the apartment and into her father's house in Massachusetts. This was no simple task. As I've said before, the large apartment was littered from floor to ceiling with God only knows what. It was reminiscent of those pictures you see of the homes of people who hoard. Clothes were piled up to three and four feet deep and the general clutter was everywhere. Her father helped as much as possible, but in the end, half of it was left for the landlord to clean up.

Kristen spent most of the months of January and February with her father, and life was quiet. Ah, such beautiful silence. No phone calls, not a word. No traumas. But we knew it would end… and soon. We suspected Tom and Alicia would never allow Kristen to live with them on a permanent basis. We waited for another phone call. I was becoming more and more anxious as the weeks went by and we hadn't heard anything from Kristen. Maybe she would stay with Tom. What a dreamer I was. On March 4 at about 1:30 p.m., Kristen called my cellphone. I remember the date well, because we had just finished lunch at a Cracker Barrel and were continuing our drive home from a fabulous, restful, ten-day vacation in New Bern, NC.

"Hi Mom. I'm coming home!"

"When?"

"Now."

I dropped my phone between the van door and my seat. The landscape moving past at seventy mph seemed to speed up and blur into oblivion as my hand groped around for my phone. I don't remember what I said next, and it really doesn't matter. The reality was she was coming home and would be there within hours. I think I told her where a house key could be found and when we would arrive some four hours or so later. As the call ended, I rolled my seat back, closed my eyes and thought, *Well, you couldn't say I didn't ask for it.*

In retrospect, it was a relief to know Kristen would be coming home to recover her life and get the help she needed. It was a process I felt in the back of my mind would take about five years. I guess I got that number from the fact that experts say it takes five years to get over any major trauma such as a divorce or loss of a spouse. But each journey starts with one day and one step and the ability to learn from the past, live in the present, and plan for the future.

During the next four hours, William and I went over some of the logistics of Kristen coming home. We lived in a three-story, three-bedroom townhouse, with two half-baths, two great rooms, and a separate living room and dining area. Kristen would occupy one of the bedrooms. On the ground floor, where we had our desks and computers, there was ample room to accommodate Kristen's desk. William would put up some shelves for her books, and her desk would fit nicely into an unused corner. Our desks were off in another corner across the room, where we wouldn't be bothering each other.

In this same space was a sitting area and an entertainment center with a large-screen TV, which Kristen could claim for her own, since our main sitting area was on the second floor in the kitchen/family room area. Having an extra person in the house wouldn't incur a major inconvenience as far as space was concerned.

"There are a few rules you have to remember now that you are living with us. First, no smoking in the house. Second, you are on your own for fixing your breakfast and lunch, but you will be expected to eat dinner with us. Third, you will need to keep your room neat."

She agreed. *That was easy. Hah.*

During our first meal together, I said our usual prayers, which consisted of more than just a simple grace. We were thankful, but we also prayed for certain people in need, asked for favors such as safe travel, and usually ended with a sentence or two reminding us to help others. Finally, there was the wrap-up, Amen. Kristen would bow her head, but never say Amen.

I guess as a pastor this annoyed me, and I asked her to participate by saying Amen. She wouldn't. It was the first, but not last, instance of disagreement. And so, we began the dance of learning to live with each other's likes, dislikes, quirks, and whimsy, which goes on to this day. There would be many adjustments to each of our ways of existing. Looking back, it was almost a year before we began to grasp the emotional drain we were experiencing with Kristen back at home.

Although William and I agreed on having Kristen come home to get help and recover, it was a mind thing in the beginning, not an emotional thing - like the first time you get on a roller coaster. You have no idea what the ride is going to be like. You soon find out that you should hang on and let the screams come and go as the dips and curves terrorize you. At last, you come to those last 200 feet, when the ride ends and you put your heart back where it belongs. It would have been lovely if the journey with Kristen was only full of gentle curves taken at a reasonable speed. But that was not to be.

FINDING KRISTEN

I'm not quite sure who we were expecting when Kristen came home, but whoever it was, it wasn't who we got. There was no rationality to her. She slept a great deal of time. In her waking hours, she was like a lost child. We hadn't seen Kristen in almost three months and she had lost considerable weight. The 150 lbs. on her tall frame left no room for an ounce of fat. Her wavy, honey-colored hair was almost down to her waist, rarely combed, like some wild woman. Her eyes were doe's eyes in oncoming headlights. There was rarely a smile on her face, only the blankness of a clean sheet of paper. She was in a state of mind where it was difficult, or impossible, for her to make any decisions.

"Mom, should I take my pills now?"

"Yes, dear."

"I don't know if I should call Annie or not."

"If you want to, I think she would enjoy that."

"William, can I go downstairs and watch TV?"

These were simple things not really requiring much thought,

or permission. What was apparent was the fact that she wanted us to help her.

"Mom, I need help. I need help. I don't know what to do now."

"I know, I know. We'll get you some help. I promise."

For a while, it was a great guessing game. When you haven't lived with a person for some thirteen years, you forget habits and may even lose the basic knowledge of what that person is like. We had last lived together with Kristen when she was a rebellious young adult of twenty-one and our history together ended there. We had no current history with her to provide a basis for understanding where her heart and mind were. Living with a thirty-four-year-old adult, particularly one who has numerous neurological problems that have never been fully sorted out and dealt with in any purposeful or useful manner, was a new challenge.

After a week of aimlessly wandering around the house, getting up, dressing, eating, saying little, moving through the space of our three floors like one walking on the moon, Kristen was making no progress in getting any help of any kind. I came home from church one day as Kristen was opening the refrigerator and grabbing a container of yogurt. I gave her a hug, grabbed my own yogurt, and gently guided her to the sofa in our upstairs great room, turned on the fireplace, and made us each a nice hot cup of tea in the microwave. Then I took her hands in mine, looked her in the face with my most pastoral expression, and cleared my throat.

"Honey, you've asked for help, but it seems you're not quite sure what to do. I need you to help me figure out how we should move forward."

"I know, Mom. I just don't know anyone here, and I don't know where to go."

"Do you know what kind of help you need?"

"I guess I need to see a doctor, but I don't know who."

"Do you think you need to see someone to talk to about life in general? Maybe a counselor?"

"Yeah. That might be good. Can you find me someone?"

"Sure. We'll work on it together. I'll try to get you an appointment with our primary care doctor, and we can go from there. I'm sure he will be able to refer us to the right people."

We eventually came to an understanding that at least for the time being, I would take charge of her life in terms of making appointments for her and driving her to the appointments with doctors, counselors, etc. We even agreed that I would initially sit in on her doctor appointments to be sure any information conveyed to them was accurate and to make sure this was the right doctor for her. In addition, I wanted to protect her if there was ever any issue about her being transgender. I wanted her to be safe. Remember, this was 2003, and gender dysphoria was not the open subject it is today in 2017.

The first thing I learned was that it wasn't a simple matter to take charge, call people, and make appointments. There were many other things to be accomplished, the first of which was to get her healthcare coverage. This was before the Affordable Care Act, and private insurance was unaffordable. Medicaid was the first thing that came to mind. While I had never dealt with any of the state agencies, I learned quickly out of necessity.

As a pastor, I knew the trauma counselor at our local community center who handled many of the indigent people and low-income families with a variety of funding and services. I called her and explained my situation. She was most helpful and led me to the Department of Child and Family Services, which just happened to be a few blocks from my church. As with any bureaucratic agency, there were forms upon forms to fill out and interviews upon interviews to be held. We were exceptionally fortunate that we were assigned a wonderful case worker who was patient with our ignorance and helpful in guiding us through the maze and mystery of the system. It was a system with which we would become intimate partners over the coming years.

Within a week, I had managed to get Kristen on food stamps and Medicaid, but that was only the tip of the iceberg. Even some doctors often hesitated to treat someone with related transgender issues. I recall one endocrinologist who was visibly concerned about prescribing hormone therapy for a transgender woman. It was clear from our first visit that she was uncomfortable in Kristen's presence. She wouldn't look Kristen in the eye and kept her head down. When she spoke, it was only to me in a soft whisper, as if she was conveying something confidential Kristen shouldn't hear. It reminded me of families talking to doctors about the patient as if she/he weren't there but is lying two feet away in the bed. She initially refused to give us minimal hormone prescriptions, but I prevailed upon her and she consented. The next time we visited, she was even more reluctant to treat Kristen, so we ended the relationship then and there. It was obvious she didn't understand a transgender's hormonal needs, and we required someone who did.

As an additional requirement to receive state assistance, one must go through a job search training program and then begin to pound the pavement in search of employment. Kristen dutifully attended the mandatory training class and then there was nothing. She would sit at the kitchen table and spend hours poring over the newspaper looking for jobs, circling possibilities, even making a phone call or two. But then nothing happened. She never went for an interview.

We coached her, prodded her, and became angry with her lack of accomplishment with even the simplest task of making an appointment for an interview. William even helped her put together a nice resume she could leave with potential employers or send to them. Still nothing. The resumes sat on the sideboard by the kitchen table. Kristen continued to sleep a great deal of time, watch TV, occasionally wash some clothes, and appear for dinner each evening. She still wouldn't say Amen. There was something basically amiss, but it was impossible for us to give it a name.

Meanwhile, with the healthcare coverage issue settled, working our way through the medical morass was another frustrating aspect of taking care of Kristen. Her diagnosis of narcolepsy at age fifteen was a good place to begin. We found a neurologist who accepted Medicaid (acceptance being another barrier to healthcare access) and then discovered it would take five months before he could see her. Fortunately, in the interim her primary care provider ordered a sleep and nap study at the local hospital in preparation for the visit with the neurologist. Even that appointment took three months to make. I could see how one could die waiting to see a specialist.

We also found making an appointment with a state agency counselor took five months. This appointment was coupled with an appointment with the resident psychiatrist, a necessary step to obtaining an anti-depressant. Fortunately, our primary care physician agreed to take her on as a patient immediately, a huge blessing because he worked with Kristen to get the many tests that she needed much sooner.

Would we ever find a real Kristen hidden behind her wall of confusion? Each day, she woke up in some kind of stupor and confusion about what to do next. She was happy to stay at home and be led from one doctor to the next or from one test to the next. Our primary care physician was unable to work with her gender issues, and our physician search continued for an endocrinologist who would prescribe her hormones, estrogen, and spironalactone to suppress her testosterone. It was another three or four months for that initial appointment.

Wait. Wait. Wait.

Here in the safety of our home, Kristen could unwrap herself, pick apart the pieces, and begin to find out not only who she was, but what she was and what she wasn't. It was the what she wasn't that was the most problematic, not only for her, but for all of us. Unpacking all this baggage put her gender issues on a very, very back burner.

Kristen, as I've mentioned before, is a very intelligent person. She knows things about physics and the universe that only most PhD's understand. One evening, we were having dinner with a friend of mine who had studied astronomy. I was captivated when she and Kristen carried on a lengthy conversation about black holes, then went on to discuss the atmospheric pressure on the moon, and ended up discussing the composition of the gas rings around Saturn. She is even a member of SETI (Search for Terrestrial Intelligence), which sweeps the universe with a variety of instruments.

One day, she explained to me the entire workings of a bomb calorimeter. She sucks up information and thirsts for knowledge. Beyond that, she rarely does anything with either her knowledge or her skills. Who is this extraordinary person with so many complex issues and such a myriad of physical and emotional streams comprising the thread of her life, all at the same time?

In perhaps the first six to eight months after Kristen came to live with us, I literally made every appointment for her: the primary care physician, the endocrinologist, the dentist, her case worker, any tests requested, such as a chest X-ray or an MRI. In addition, I attended every medical appointment with her and acted as her medical advocate, a job I still do to this day from time to time. During our second or third visit to her neurologist, we were sitting in two chairs opposite Dr. Mueller's large desk, cluttered high with folders and assorted papers, listening to his report on Kristen's sleep study, trying to keep up with his litany of technical terms. Behind his desk was a wall to wall, ceiling to floor bookcase filled to overflowing with books and family photos.

"She failed all her nap tests, and her REM time is off the

charts. She goes into REM within minutes, while a normal person takes over twenty minutes and up." He handed us the report.

"So, what does this all mean?"

"She has one of the worst cases of narcolepsy I have ever seen."

I sat there picking at my fingers, wondering where to go with this information.

He continued, "There is not much of anything that can be done about it, since research on sleep issues has only begun in the past twenty years. No cause, no cure. I'm sorry."

"Really? Nothing?"

"We can give her medication to help her stay awake during the day and medication to help her sleep at night, but even that will not give her a normal sleep cycle. She has no circadian rhythm, and medication can only do so much."

We'd known she had narcolepsy since she was fifteen-years-old in 1983 when an endocrinologist diagnosed it. But other than the diagnosis and some stimulants, we never knew the depths of this disease. She had never had a sleep study before. My hopes for her future dimmed as I envisioned a life of eternal dependency. Although it was our blessing when we found Dr. Mueller, the head of the sleep clinic at our local hospital, and well-respected, he really offered little substantive help.

He tossed Kristen's report folder on his desk, put his arms

behind his head, leaned back in his chair, and in an offhand manner said, “Why isn’t Kristen applying for Social Security Supplemental Income? She obviously can’t work with such a severe case of narcolepsy.”

Really? Kristen and I swiveled around in our chairs, our eyes meeting in a swirl of puzzlement. The notion that she couldn’t work at all was as surprising to both of us as waking up to find the sun hadn’t risen.

It was always our intention as soon as Kristen got her medical and drug-related issues under control that she would return to some type of work. But to not be able to work was something we never even whispered in all these thirty-five years. Kristen confided in me how she always had difficulty keeping jobs, sometimes quitting after a few months when the pressure of being on time got to be too much or often being fired due to repeated falling asleep on the job in the middle of the day. Still, she had managed to work. This new twist would have to be worked out. When the medical issues were under control, it was time to get back to our case worker to apply for state disability supplement and on to the nightmare of the Social Security Administration to apply for disability insurance. I don’t know whether finding Kristen was better or worse than finding our way through the SSI system, but that rabbit hole is not one I am willing to jump into right now. Suffice it to say that after almost four years, she was denied those benefits.

Meanwhile, as each day, week, and month passed, Kristen began to gather her strength and wits. She was on appropriate medications, tending to her health, and willing to venture out on her own. In fact, she was finding her way around the city of Philadelphia, a thirty-five-minute drive, and giving us a different kind of concern. A different picture of a Kristen I never knew.

Philadelphia, and later New York City, helped Kristen understand and develop one of her great talents as a photographer. In fact, for two years, it was a hopeful time that she would find her niche in the world and could make a living doing something she loved and at which she was very good. At first, her forays into the big city of Philadelphia were to get away from the confines of home and family and the agony of her struggle with her gender and her physical and neurological issues.

She had always loved to dance, we learned, and the dance club scene was her outlet for this aspect of her personality. She made some friends and looked forward to her weekends in the big city. For us, it represented the drug scene, criminals, prostitutes, and God only knows what else. As it turned out, these trips did give Kristen an opportunity to continue her drug use, and she openly admitted using Ecstasy from time to time.

To say we were deeply troubled by her activities would be an understatement. I always worried when she didn't show up for a couple of days. Being transgender posed enough of an issue, along with her narcolepsy. Did someone hurt her? Did she fall asleep at the wheel and die in an accident? Did she take drugs? Die of an overdose? A mother's mind has a fertile imagination. In my case, these were real possibilities.

One Sunday morning, we got a call from Kristen. She was in a hospital in Philadelphia. Apparently, she had passed out in the street the night before and some kind soul picked her up and took her to the local hospital. She remembered nothing of what happened, but this episode only served to sharpen my concern about her well-being.

One night, delighted by the club lights, she took her camera. This launched her into an attempt to become a club photographer and sell her photographic art. She took stunning photos of the colorful club lights, flashing strobes on the twisting, dancing bodies below. The pictures were unique examples of abstract art, and many were used for publicity and advertising by clubs in both Philadelphia and New York. The lighting she captured was brilliant as she climbed up into the catwalks in clubs to get just the right angle, just the right light. Her eye for the extraordinary was itself extraordinary. I'm not a lover of abstract art, but I love her club photos.

Unfortunately, there was never the income flow that would have enabled her to support herself. Expenses just to get to the city and back were reimbursed, but whenever she suggested that she should be paid for her pictures, people stopped asking her to take pictures for their advertising. Two years later, our family moved to southern Delaware, which put Philadelphia more than a two-hour drive away from home and New York City almost five hours away. As fuel costs soared and with no income, driving to those cities became an economic impossibility for us to fund her trips. Further, with her narcolepsy causing her to stop and take frequent naps, a two-hour trip often became an eight-hour trip. By the middle of 2006, Kristen's trips to the city were ended, and her hopes of being a famous club photographer dashed upon the rocks of frustration. It was a disappointment for all of us.

Finding Kristen, knowing Kristen, sorting out Kristen often drained my emotional resources. Even as I write this book I sometimes put my head down on the pages and simply weep, tears coming from unknown depths in my soul. She is on this journey forever; and so long as I live, I will always walk her walk with her. It's what a mother does, at least in my mind.

NO GOING BACK

It has now been over thirteen years since Kristen came home to live with us, and it is a reality that she is not here for a visit. There was no recovery period in the sense that she was purged of her drug use, stopped partying, and was no longer hanging around with the wrong crowd. There was no recovery period when she would find her sea legs and again be off onto the road of self-sufficiency, when she would find full-time employment and be able to find her own apartment somewhere, cook her own meals, iron her own clothes, and pay her own bills. It just wasn't happening.

Quite often, the subject of Kristen's surgery came up, either between her and me or between me and her father. I'm never sure why it keeps coming up, but it does, rather like a bad penny that simply won't get lost in the melee of life. There is a mystique about having the sex reassignment surgery, or genital reconstructive surgery (GRS), as it is called. We look at it from two perspectives. The first, which is the one we discuss most, is whether Kristen really wants to have the surgery. One day it is a definite "yes," and the next day a definite "maybe." However, it is never a "no."

If gender dysphoria is all about being born in the wrong gender body, why wouldn't it be a priority to change that? From my perspective, I am completely puzzled by the fact she has even a moment of hesitation. Why wouldn't she want to have the complete feminine body she longs to have as soon as possible?

The other aspect of our conversations about GRS is generally about the cost (which while somewhat prohibitive, is coming down year after year) and the physiology of the surgery itself. We have talked about going to Thailand for the surgery where it is commonplace and relatively inexpensive, even including airfare and hotels. As of this writing, there has been no decision one way or the other and the excuse is always the same – no money. Well, that's not exactly true because, although our funds are limited, there is always a way to finance medical needs crucial to one's success in life. I guess when Kristen finally decides this is a must in her life, we will find the means.

It is said that most transgender people never have the reassignment surgery for a variety of reasons. Cost, fear, and perhaps no need, depending on one's sexual behavior and other relationships. Some transgender people are also much older when they acknowledge they have gender identity issues and simply don't care one way or the other. I do know it isn't for lack of information. Back in the early 1990's when we first learned of Kristen's gender identity issues, there was little or nothing published on the subject. Today, there are many books and personal stories available, as well as the Internet. Amazon lists over 36,000 items, from books to videos to clothing. A Google search of transgender yields over eighty-seven million hits. Yes, there's lots of information out there today.

I'm not convinced that cost is the only barrier. When Kristen first came to live with us, we offered to match any income she made dollar for dollar to help accelerate her funds for her surgery. Well, she sold some family collectibles her father had given her on eBay and we matched those funds. But that was it. She has not held a job since August of 2002. She has some funds sitting in the bank, waiting.

So, that didn't work. Then, about three years ago, I offered to sell a valuable sculpture I have in order to pay for her surgery. In my mind, I thought if she had her surgery, that would be one less thing on her mind. I also thought it might make it easier for her to assimilate herself into the world as fully female. However, the deal was that she would have to contact one of the auction houses and find out the details of how we might go about making that happen. Nothing happened. Finally, I asked her again if she really wanted the surgery. She told me that quite frankly, she was somewhat afraid of the surgery.

"Afraid of what, Kristen?"

"Afraid the surgery will turn out badly, I guess."

"We'll be sure we get a good surgeon. We'll check his work."

"That will cost too much."

Fear and cost, a cycle she falls back on each time the subject comes up. Financing a sex-change orientation surgery is certainly a major barrier to making that final decision, as is the fear of the unknown. The cost, however, is coming down and is now close to half what it was ten years ago. At least once a year, I ask Kristen if she has ever regretted her decision to live her life openly as the interior woman she is. Her answer is unwaveringly the same – No! And it continues to be no although she lives on the edges of society as a Tranny.

I've learned that regardless of the consequences of being called a freak, fearing for her life or being socially isolated, she is a woman and her body is her prison, not her persona. As her mother, it is one of the saddest weights I carry in my heart and soul, for what loving mother does not want the very best for her child?

I am angry that this gentle, sensitive, talented, beautiful daughter cannot live peacefully in a slender, graceful, female body. A friend once told me she thought it was the cruelest trick of nature to put one sex in the body of the opposite gender. I couldn't agree more. I was never angry at God, as some might have been, because I knew this was one of those developmental situations that, probably, could never have been prevented. Nor do I believe it could have been predicted.

Perhaps someday science will have the tools and talents to figure out this mystery, just not in my lifetime. In fact, even with sex reassignment surgery and extensive cosmetic surgery, her body would never be completely feminine. It's one of those things that would have to be changed in utero. When I think about all the advances that science has made in the past century, I'm confident that it will happen someday. Sadly, I don't believe it will be in time to help my Kristen.

Today, however, I believe there is a way to help ease the misery of this situation, and that is to have sex reassignment surgery paid for by insurance companies. To be transgender is as debilitating for an individual as any other illness, deformity, or disability. Billions of dollars are spent on helping make people physically whole from any number of issues. Being transgender is also psychically debilitating and cannot be helped with psychoanalysis, only with surgery and hormone replacement therapy. In fact, recently the family of a transgender person described the condition as being a birth defect. A valid assumption, one might say, in light of the fact that each of these people is born this way. They are born into a world that says this is not a normal human condition. Yet it is denied by almost every insurance company, leaving a host of young people with great futures trapped in bodies not their own, living in misery rather than living productive and happy lives.

There is hope. California is now the first state to pay for reassignment surgery for prison inmates. It is amazing to me how this might be the first opening in the door for insurers outside the prison system to offer the same coverage for all transgender people.

Three years ago at Christmas, I decided there was one thing I could afford to do that might help Kristen feel more feminine. I gave her laser hair removal sessions to remove every hair on her body (except her head, of course). She was ecstatic. But the most remarkable part of it all is how her attitude about herself has changed. She now reflects a more confident, relaxed woman. She wears shorts and short-sleeve blouses. She is no longer afraid to wear a low-cut top with some pretty jewelry. She sits outside and tans herself in the summer and I can just sense that if nothing else, she is more comfortable in her new, hairless, skin. I call her my hairless Chihuahua. We both laugh. Maybe the next thing I can afford is to give her are new breasts. While her hormone therapy has developed her breasts a bit, they are still rather small. With her large frame, a size D cup would be more proportional than a B cup.

Kristen is still waiting to have sex reassignment surgery to give her female genitals. It is scary to her, as she fears she will lose her male sexual desire as a woman or never experience sexual pleasure again. I have come to accept that it is also scary to me because it is so final. Almost daily, I still wonder what if she made a mistake. After surgery, there would be no going back. No being him again.

Removing, reshaping, or changing a part of our body, whether we feel it is appropriate to our gender or not, is a serious consideration. After all, we have lived with a particular body our entire life. Further, there is a wide range of outcomes with respect to the surgery itself. Some of it is excellent, while other procedures don't produce a very attractive or successful result. Taking that final step for Kristen is fraught with "what ifs" and unfortunately, those questions can't always be answered and/or guaranteed.

Yet it can't be easy for her not having the curves, the sensuality, and the gentleness of the feminine body she so desires. She keeps a book of Vargas pin-ups in her room just to admire the beauty of the female body she will never have. I can only imagine her daily pain living like this. In truth, I can't even imagine that degree of longing. It isn't all about pronouns, names, makeup, surgery, or dress. It's about a life yearning to be lived.

BEING A GIRL

Since that first night when we met "Wendy," my Kristen has struggled with what to wear and how to apply makeup. Well, at least as her mother, I think she has. After living with us full time for over thirteen years now, she has slowly but steadily improved in her choice of clothing and makeup, but not without some contention between us. After years of confrontation about too much makeup and the appearance it projected, too tight clothing and the image of wanting sex from every male that walked by, I think I have finally figured it out. Some of it anyway.

Girls growing up watch mom put on make-up and get dressed for one occasion or another. I remember many times sitting on the closed toilet seat watching my naked mother putting on her makeup for a fancy evening out with my stepfather. I used to giggle as she raised her eyebrows to put on eyebrow pencil or pursed her lips just before she smacked them between a tissue to remove the excess. Her makeup was always subtle, but complete, from her eyebrows to her lips. And while she wore bright red lipstick, she never looked hard or cheap. I rarely watched her get dressed, but I remember vividly her stepping out of her bedroom in one beautiful dress or gown after another over the years. She looked stunning and gorgeous, like a queen in my childlike eyes. I learned over the years how certain dressier clothes are worn at night and to parties, while more conservative dress was worn to church. Hats were worn during the day, never at night.

My daughter, Holly, used to watch me put on my makeup, use my curling iron to curl my hair, and often helped me pick out just the right outfit for an occasion. Girls learn through osmosis that mom doesn't wear makeup to the supermarket and wears jeans and tee but dresses up and puts a bit of makeup on to go out to lunch. Evening affairs and cocktail parties require all-out makeup and dressy dresses or slacks with a beautiful top.

I can remember my own mother saying things to me like, "Where do you think you are going in that outfit?" when I would be wearing an inappropriate dress or jeans or shorts or something. I can also remember her saying, "You march right into the bathroom and take that makeup off!"

She didn't have to give me a specific reason because I knew it meant I had too much on. One day when I was about to go out in a pair of short shorts, she didn't let me get past the front door.

"You only wear those at the beach," she admonished.

And off they came and a more decent pair of Bermuda shorts were put on.

While it took me some time to come to this understanding, I now realize Kristen, being Christopher until she was over thirty years old, never grew up being a girl. That is to say, I never mothered her into understanding how girls dressed or put on makeup. She didn't have those subtle, or maybe not so subtle, gentle or not so gentle, directions, hints, admonitions, and outright orders about what to do about her appearance.

Maybe better late than never. Maybe. Easier said than done when you are confronting someone who is in her mid-forties and already thinks she knows everything. Subtlety has to be the order of the day. For example, Kristen always makes her eyebrows way too fat. One day, we had a conversation about bone shaving her brow bones because men have more prominent brow bones than women. Several days thereafter, I mentioned to her that if she would make her eyebrows thinner, it would make her brow look less prominent. Voila! Thinner eyebrows.

Another time, William commented that a sweater she was wearing looked a bit small on her. Blessedly, he didn't say it made her look fat! The next thing I knew the too-tight sweater was in the Donate box on its way to the local thrift shop.

And speaking of thrift shops, that is where Kristen does almost all of her clothes shopping. Gratefully, it saves her a ton of money, but it also gives her the opportunity to buy a variety of clothes in a variety of sizes and see what looks good or doesn't.

One day, Kristen came into the living room in an all-pink outfit, full of frills and ruffles, too tight, too short, and about what you might find on a five-year-old playing ballerina. Without missing a beat, I said, "You're not going outside in that are you?"

It was the first time I had ever said that out loud, but I just couldn't help myself.

"No, mom, I'm not, but I never got a chance to dress like this when I was little and I like to know how it feels."

Kristen, bless her heart, was just being that five-year old girl.

Just remembering that makes me want to cry.

Another issue has been her breasts. For her size, they are small, even with the addition of female hormones. At some point, she will get breast implants. Until then, it's all about padded bras and what we used to call falsies. She has them in a variety of sizes, and I never know whether she is going to be Mae West or Twiggy. When we attended a family reunion spanning about four days, I did suggest that she pick a boob size and stick with it for the entire time. Gratefully, she agreed.

And so, it goes for her. Some days, she dresses like the mature woman she is in the correct size, nothing hanging out, flattering age-appropriate styles. Other days, well, who knows - she could be two or seven or ten or sixteen, wearing tights with a tutu, or large pink flowers on a top, pink polka dots on her tights, flashing, glowing lights on sneakers, or a mini-skirt that barely covers her crotch, no tights, stiletto heels, and a tube top in size 0. We never know, but she does have the good sense not to go outside the house. I guess the hardest part was understanding. The next hardest part was communication. My slip of the tongue led to her honesty and now we both have a better understanding of some of her transgender clothing issues.

Other aspects of being a female manifest themselves in behavior as well. Just recently, she walked past the kitchen sink, cleared her throat, and spit in the sink. I told her that a lady wouldn't do that. Well, it was if I had cut off her hand! In not so many words, she told me that she never wanted me to tell her how to be a female.

There are many of her mannerisms that are distinctly male, such as sitting in a chair with her legs spread apart. And while I would love to be her mother and bring her up like a girl even at this late stage, I find that I must bite my tongue. I feel such sadness at these times and my heart is heavy. I so want her to be the woman she is, but I also must learn to accept the fact that some of her habits will always be male. I imagine this is the case for many transgender folks.

We are the product not only of our genetic makeup, but of our environment and what we have learned along the way from our experiences. In reality, transgender people will always be the part male, part female they carry within them. I guess like people can never change the color of their skin, transgender folks will never completely change their gender habits, mannerism, and ingrained learnings.

THE ARTISTE

The shining star that is Kristen shines brighter since she discovered the enormous artistic talent she has creating oil and acrylic paintings. One of my favorites is of the gazebo straddling the pond in the backyard. I asked her to do it for me, and gave her a photo I had taken. I expected this bright, sunny painting with the pond edged in orange-speckled tiger lilies. What I got was a gorgeous painting of the gazebo at sunset, washed in that subtle glow that only comes from God at the end of the day. It is in the style of the old masters and gathers many compliments from our visitors. Where her talent came from is just another one of those mysteries that constitute this complex person. One day, she wandered into the dining room and said, "Mom, I want to join the Rehoboth Art League and take oil painting lessons."

Well, where did that come from?

However, since she was becoming more and more reclusive, I thought it was a great idea to get her out and about and into the world of the living. She was immediately signed up as a member and registered for her first class in plein air impressionistic painting in oils. Quite honestly, I didn't know what to expect. I remembered years ago, she had done some charcoal sketches that were much more than your kindergarten art. She had also taken an art class at about age ten or eleven and painted a lovely little girl holding a bouquet, done with acrylics. It was so good I even had it framed. It now hangs in her room.

Before her class began, we bought her what seemed like an overwhelming supply of brushes, paints, media, and canvases. As was typical of her, she needed to have a complete complement of whatever it was she was undertaking before beginning a new venture. We even bought a taboret and three banks of small artist supply drawers.

Before her class, she crafted an incredible easel out of old tripod parts. Her inventive mind is something to behold when she begins to create something she needs. In the end, however, it turned out to be too heavy to use as a portable easel for outdoor use. We found a suitable portable easel in one of the art catalogs, as well as a portable stool in one of the sport stores. She was now ready for her class.

Wanting to experiment a bit with oils, she decided to try an oil painting of the aforementioned gazebo in our back yard. The gazebo, she said, was going to become her water lilies, referring to the plethora of water lilies that Monet painted from his home in Giverney, France. And off she went, dressed in a white lab coat, a pink beret, and her painting gear. For a very first oil painting, it was remarkable in the vivid detail of the gazebo, particularly the cedar shingles and the reflection of the railing in the pond. We were impressed at the time with her initial talent and encouraged her to continue.

Another favorite painting of mine is one that she painted in Acadia National Park near Bar Harbor, Maine. During our summer vacation in 2012, Kristen asked if we could take a detour and go to Acadia, because she wanted to paint something there. Although it was almost 800 miles out of the way, I agreed. Being retired, we didn't have any time restraints. It's also a lovely part of our world, and it would be nice to see it again. We arrived on a Wednesday evening and spent all day Thursday looking for just the right scene for her to paint. One didn't have the right light. Another had too many rocks, a third had no mountain. I was beginning to think the perfect spot would never appear out of the Maine mist.

Anyone who's been there knows there are literally hundreds of wonderful scenes to paint, but Kristen wanted to paint something that wasn't ordinary and hadn't been painted a thousand times. We've all seen those Maine scenes of rocky shores with crashing waves, serene, sailboat filled harbors, picturesque lighthouses, or lobster pots piled next to a shack. I should have known she wouldn't be happy painting those. She always wants to be unique.

Duck Creek was up a lightly traveled road and had been recommended to Kristen by one of the park rangers she queried. It was an absolutely beautiful scene with Sergeant Mountain in the background. There was even an interesting beaver house in the middle of a small stream as an object of interest to be captured. We walked around for over an hour just looking for the right spot for Kristen to set up the next day. We found a nice hummock of land under a tree that was as perfect as if it sat right in the middle of a Lilliputian meadow, rimmed by the forest and Maine's low-slung coastal mountains. It was a hidden gem. The wildflowers were in bloom, the trees were full and luscious; and for a mid-summer day, it was not exceptionally hot. The reflection of the deep blue sky on the stream made the water look almost Caribbean aqua. The shadows in the afternoon provided just the right amount of light contrast. Yes, almost perfect.

At 1:00 p.m. the next day, Kristen was all set up and ready to paint. We left her there with a supply of water and enough equipment to paint the world. We then traipsed off to take a windjammer cruise off Bar Harbor. She would be there without interruption to paint for the afternoon.

As we were enjoying a late afternoon cup of coffee after our cruise, a text message came in from Kristen asking us to bring her a soda. Off we went to purchase same and take it to her. It was 4:30 p.m. As we arrived, I was very disappointed. The painting looked as if it was just beginning: sketched, but not even beginning to have the fullness of a complete oil painting. There was a lot of streaky green on the canvass in a variety of hues, but no depth, and not a hint of the blue water or sky. The yellow wildflowers on the bank of the creek were like charcoal sticks, waiting for that burst of color they wore. The sun was playing nip and tuck with the horizon, and it seemed impossible she would ever finish it in the next two hours. She asked us to come back and get her at 7:00 p.m., which meant a very late dinner, but hey, she was "The Artiste." Who were we to stop the flow of those creative juices?

When we returned promptly at 7:00 p.m., she had produced what I consider to be one of the best she has done so far. She posts some of her paintings on Facebook, and we display a few pieces in our great room. Several people have asked to buy this painting. However, it is ours, Kristen says, because we took her up there and paid for the trip.

Later, she told us that when we brought her the soda, she was filled with despair because the painting was not coming together as she hoped and she didn't think she would finish it. I think Kristen learned a lesson in perseverance that afternoon beside Duck Creek. I know it awed me.

The most important aspect of Kristen's painting talent has

been the effect it has had on her confidence. Her successes in life pale in comparison to her failures. But the talent that shows in her paintings has surprised many and brought accolade after accolade into her life, something she had rarely experienced.

You know, when you walk into someone's home and admire a painting, you expect that people will say, "Oh, how nice," or "What a wonderful piece," just to be polite. But when people who see her work in our home and don't know it's hers comment on how much they like it, you know it's good. When we tell them it is Kristen's and she has only been painting a couple of years, they are astonished at her talent.

She has already sold two of her paintings and is continuing to take classes and learn. Her favorites are abstracts, but she also experiments with different media, painting on glass or tinfoil, for example. Florals are a favorite, from some miniatures to a larger piece. Although she started with landscapes, they are not her favorite subject and I doubt she will produce her one thousand gazebos. Kristen also goes in for the unusual, and one of her better paintings is an acrylic of a large, intense, aqua-marine eye – up close and personal. I had to put that one away. It was so realistic I felt like someone was always watching me over my shoulder. She once even painted a big set of lips just for fun.

Life with a transgender child can sometimes be so focused on that one aspect of his or her character we forget to see and appreciate all the other parts that make up a unique human being: the talents, flaws, joys, sadnesses, quirks, quarks, and personalities. We only see the trans issues, not the entire complexity of our child's life. I believe through Kristen's painting; her soul is soaring. As her mother, I soar with her. In so doing, her transgender struggles and joys are put aside, for a moment or two at least. More than anything, I keep reminding myself that there is much, much more to my Kristen than her gender. Much more.

CHANGE

This book is peppered with that word. It is wrapped around our heart throughout this journey with Kristen's transgender transition, as well as her other issues. There are many words – love, joy, fear, uncertainty, laughter, acceptance, questioning, understanding, confusion – the list goes on and on. But if I had to pick one word that typifies this process it would have to be change.

I have always considered myself a person who embraces change. I experienced change very early in my life when my father served in World War II and we moved three times just after my fifth birthday. When I was six, my parents separated and divorced, and my mother and I moved from Michigan to Arizona to live with my grandparents. Finally, my mother remarried two months before my seventh birthday and we moved to California. In two short years, my life was radically changed. My father was given custody of my Down Syndrome sister and my family was not only torn apart, but split in two. Thereafter, I only saw my sister and my father at most twice a year and usually only once a year.

Since that time, I have developed a kind of roll-with-the-punches attitude toward change. If we start on the micro level for example, our landscape changes daily. The wrinkles in our pajamas are never the same. We never sleep exactly the same number of minutes each night. A bar of soap never gets used up in exactly the same number of uses. Small, tiny changes that we don't ever notice.

Macro changes are ones we rarely forget: a death, a birth, a marriage, a baptism, an accident, cancer, a presidential assassination, a graduation, a coming out, a transgender transition. The majority of changes in our life happen in between the micro and the macro changes. While Kristen's transgender transition was a major change in our life, to say the least, within that change were a series of smaller changes. Changes like name changes, clothing changes, makeup, pronouns, and telling friends and family. At every turn of the transgender corner, there was one change or the other.

How did we all deal with all these changes? It must be acknowledged that Kristen herself went through the biggest emotional upheaval during this major change in her life. At the early age of perhaps five, she struggled with her identity and her desire to be surrounded by female things such as jewelry, clothing, and even girlfriends. She struggled with the terror and uncertainty of telling her family. I like to think that she chose to tell me first, because I do handle change well. It was safe. Telling her father was not so safe. As it turned out, he didn't handle this change as easily.

Tom, I think, has had the hardest time dealing with this major change in his life. I remember that in the earliest years of Kristen's coming out to us, we held conference calls with him, her stepmother, her stepfather, and myself. We would talk for hours. In addition, I would have private conversations with Tom, and I remember one in particular. It was near Christmas and I sat on the stairs going up to our bedrooms, watching the tree lights twinkle, thinking how Christmas for me always meant new life.

"Tom, why are you so hesitant to accept that Christopher is transgender? I don't get it," I said.

"I'm really confused about what all this means."

"What do you mean?"

"Well, is this a phase? Is it permanent? I don't know. It just feels all wrong."

Sighing, I said, "I don't completely understand it all myself, except I know she needs our support."

Tom, clearing his throat and taking a long pause, finally said, "I don't think you understand how I feel. I'm losing my son."

"Yes, I know. You've told me that before. I thought you had gotten over that."

Finally, I got it. I just held the phone close and let my tears flow as his answer was filled with the heartfelt yearning of a man with only one son who was losing his future heritage. It wasn't just about losing a son.

I was raised to believe for every man it was important to have a son, an heir to carry on the family name. It took Tom longer than the rest of us to accept that Christopher/Kristen never changed who she was as a person, just that she was no longer his son. For years, Tom occasionally asked if I ever thought Kristen would be Christopher again. Once, when I asked if he would help pay for her surgery, he got quiet and contemplative. I believe he feels if Kristen never gets the reassignment surgery, there is that slim hope Christopher will return to him, that he will have his son back, his heritage.

Even William's son, Matthew, and his family now know that Kristen is transgender and have welcomed her into their home when we visit for Thanksgiving. Only one friend is a homophobe, and we all know it. Kristen sensed this very early on in her transition. While there is never anything spoken, there is an air of discomfort when they are both in the same room. Mercifully for everyone concerned, we are geographically separated and there is rarely an occasion for them to be together. Blessedly, most people like Kristen for who she is through all of her changes and include her in many of our family activities. At my Aunt

Alice's ninetieth birthday party, she commented to me, "Kristen is such a sweet girl and so considerate of others."

Yes, she is.

For me, the biggest change that still gives me pause is how Kristen dresses and wears makeup. No matter what internal changes happen, it's difficult to hide or mask her male physique.

"Mom, people know I am a tranny when they look at my hands. They always give us away."

"Mom, I don't have a natural waistline like you do."

"Mom, I have broad masculine shoulders and no hips."

"Mom, while I have no Adam's apple, my voice is still too deep to be a woman."

"Mom, I have prominent brows like most men. It's one of those things that protected the caveman's eyes from the sun while out hunting. I'll have to get a brow shave."

I've come to accept she is a unique person, a transgender person, who even with some cosmetic surgery, will always have that maleness about her.

Through much prayer and talks with God, I have come to accept this flamboyantly dressed, bright-eyed, person who walks out the door with us. I try to compliment her when she looks particularly wonderful and to keep my mouth shut when I don't think she is dressing appropriately for the occasion. I remember once biting my tongue when she was dressed for lunch with friends in a tight-fitting, black lace cocktail dress that accentuated her lack of feminine features.

When I want her dress to be toned down, I always say, "Kristen, please dress conservatively for this occasion."

She knows what I mean and shows up in a nice pair of black slacks with a bright colored, loose fitting top that hides her straight waist and no hips. It's part of accepting the change that is Kristen and understanding, quite frankly, it is what it is. I keep telling myself how beautiful she is inside and that's what counts.

In the final analysis, however, it is Kristen and Kristen alone who had to go through all the changes of being transgender, the changes from the psychological testing for her transition, which must have been both laborious and yet, liberating. It is Kristen whose body had to undergo the change of her internal systems through hormone therapy. It is Kristen who has had to undergo what is an ongoing change of meeting people in the world and opening herself up to who she is as a transgender woman. And it is Kristen who, through her change, must suffer the various and different reactions and responses to her physical maleness integrated with her female persona.

While I came to understand the life of a transgender person in ways I never imagined, my struggle to deal with her gender change created my own internal ups and downs. As I learned about her public life, my dealing with her change was a speck of dust in the greater picture of her life. I knew the private Kristen. Her struggle to live publicly as a transgender woman was brutal at times, as the comments of an uninformed public assaulted her very identity. Cutting, damaging remarks.

"You faggot."

"You freak."

"You should crawl in a hole and die."

"God hates you."

I was with her one day waiting in line to pick up one of her prescriptions. This rather scruffy looking young man dressed in torn jeans, a rather dirty flannel shirt, five-o-clock shadow, dirty fingernails, and greasy hair below his shoulders walked past and said, "What are you dude, a man or a woman," in a sneering tone of voice. Kristen lowered her head and turned away. I watched her brush a tear from her eye. I glared at the man as he slunk away with a smirk on his face. I was disgusted. Who are these people? Where is their humanity? I put my arm around Kristen, my head on her shoulder, and we just stood together like that in silence for a fleeting moment. I so desperately wanted to take away her hurt and humiliation. Coping with all those changes is something none of the rest of us had to experience.

I am now at peace with these changes. I no longer worry if I should tell people or not. I simply do if there is an opportunity. I don't want to hide it, because when they meet her, I have seen the look of confusion on people's faces as they wonder if she is a man or a woman. I no longer worry Kristen will be angry if I tell someone she is transgender. She knows I do it with pride. I no longer worry Kristen will be angry with me if I suggest she wear something more appropriate or tone down her makeup. She gets it. She understands that how she presents herself with me needs, for the comfort of others, to be less, shall we say, colorful. I am much more relaxed and open about her transgender transition. I simply don't tense up as we go out in public. I no longer hesitate to invite her to go places with me. I know she is expressing herself as she wants. If I can't stand beside her, shame on me. She's my daughter. Period. And I introduce her to others as if she is the best, most beautiful daughter ever.

But let me tell you, it has been one enormous sequence of change in all our lives over the years since I first heard, "It's a boy," and she first uttered, "Mom, I'm a girl."

LIMBO

Limbo is a Roman Catholic concept of a place where babies who died and had not been baptized dwelt until, I believe, they were prayed into heaven. A kind of waiting room to see God. A kind of middle in the muddle of death between heaven and earth. I imagine it was a place of joy and happiness filled with the gurgling laughter of babies aged one hour to two years old, some kicking and squirming in cribs, others crawling around inspecting everything, and others toddling about on wobbly legs. All of them with broad grins on their faces while the sound of belly laughs filled the air. Reuben would have loved to have painted this scene.

In so many ways, Kristen lives in limbo. While Kristen's life is no longer that of a toddler and her life is not filled with continual joy and laughter, she is in a state of waiting. There is always the waiting for the surgery, and only God knows if that will ever occur. And there is the waiting to see what life holds for her in the future. It is a bleak scene filled with her transgender issues, her narcolepsy issues, and her ADD issues.

Even the success of her painting has its own limbo. While it raises her confidence and gives her a deep sense of joy and accomplishment, there are days when she cannot find the motivation to paint and waits for some "Aha" moment that will inspire her. Her room is too small for a real studio, and she waits for the day when we can either find her a studio to rent or find her some independent housing that allows for both studio and living space.

There are many limbos in Kristen's life. Her narcolepsy is degenerative; we are told – not good. Her ADD hasn't so far responded well to any of the so-called ADD drugs such as Strattera that focus her thoughts and allow her to be productive in any meaningful sense. Her sex reassignment surgery hangs in the air, waiting for both the funding and Kristen's courage to go through with it. Even her painting may have to wait. Yes, she lives in limbo. In many ways, we are all in limbo.

Finally, there is the limbo of loneliness and isolation that is Kristen's space. After her adventures in the big cities ended, it seemed that Kristen had no direction, no driving force in her life. Depression comes and goes in her life. Most troubling for me was her growing withdrawal from the world. There was a time when she was a thrift-shop-maven, going on a daily circuit of every thrift shop in lower Delaware. For a while, she even managed to spend a few hours a week volunteering, helping her favorite shop sort through donations. With her diseases, known and unknown, she spends a fair amount of time visiting hospitals and doctors, but all of this is not a substitute for a life.

Kristen spends hours in her room, rarely going out, even to practice her photography or to paint. She takes pictures of lightning and clouds and birds in the yard, but from the deck or the solarium, not from some place five or ten or fifteen miles from home. She almost never paints the gazebo in our backyard anymore, although it is only thirty feet from our deck. I feared she is becoming a recluse, a hermit. It is my prayer that her painting interests will take her beyond our place and will be her salvation, saving her from a closeted world of limbo.

Although her therapist and the family have encouraged Kristen to join some type of group, whether a social group or a support group, there is none that she felt she would be comfortable joining. I can only guess that she feels she doesn't have enough in common with other people she would meet in such groups to establish lasting friendships. Even her membership in the art league and her painting classes have not opened a new world of meeting new people and going new places. She still spends an inordinate amount of time alone.

I have heard it is difficult for people with ADD to make and keep friends anyway. Over four years ago, the townhouse next to ours was rented to a nice young couple with a small son. They are about Kristen's age. Although it happened slowly at first, she has become good friends with them. I am ever so grateful that she now has these friends to visit and share her life with. She visits them frequently, but she still spends a fair amount of time alone.

It really saddens me, and particularly so, since I have less life ahead of me than behind me and I will not be here for her within as few as perhaps five or ten years. Kristen always says, "Don't worry mom," anytime I mention my worry about her. As any mother would, I simply worry. I have always told my children that my primary job is to worry about them

I remember once I said to Kristen, "I know how I won't have to worry about you after I'm dead."

"How?" she asked.

"Five minutes before I die, I'll kill you. No worry about you, no prison for me."

We laughed about it at the time, but in the quiet worry corner of my heart, the issue of her future care when I am gone is too close to a reality to even make light of it.

But life isn't all gloom and doom and limbo. Each morning the three of us gather for breakfast, some comments about the weather, and then our puzzles. Our daily newspaper publishes three – a Sudoku, Cryptic Byword, and a crossword. Kristen is great at solving the Sudoku with her logical thinking. I suck at them. My forte are the word puzzles. William and I love the crosswords, which we do together. Each morning, Kristen and I race each other to see who finishes which puzzle first. She usually whips my fanny at Sudoku, but I'm getting better at it and have even beaten her time maybe twice. Kristen is getting much better at the Cryptic Byword and has consistently matched or beaten my time. We feel as if we are helping each other develop those weak areas in our brains. We even have penalty minutes if we must ask for help. It sets the mood for our day.

It is also during this morning time when we discuss events in the news, our thoughts on the goings on at our condo, or the latest weather report. She and William have developed an easy relationship and there hasn't been a flare-up between them in years. I think they both try very hard to avoid contention and simply walk away from each other when they see disagreement coming. I too am more at ease, since I don't worry as much about a coming storm.

In the evening, we say our prayers together before dinner and share ideas, thoughts, and happenings during this hour. Politics is a favorite topic, as is some item on the news. We watch Wheel of Fortune and Jeopardy during dinner and race each other to get the answers. We're all good at it. Kristen has taken it upon herself to be the one who clears the dishes and loads the dishwasher. We are grateful for that.

Kristen is a huge help carrying groceries and heavier items

for us as our ability to do those things for ourselves diminishes. She even drives us to events in the evenings as our eyesight fades with age. We often sit outside on our deck by the pond on a nice afternoon watching the wildlife or the clouds or discussing some event or happening of the day.

We have many, many discussions about all manner of things in the world. Some of them end up in disagreement, but usually we respect each other's diverse opinions. We go to the movies together from time to time and although our movie tastes are different, we manage to tolerate each other's choices. Occasionally, we will watch a TV show together, go for a walk, or as we did in 2011, take a six-week journey to the west coast and back.

That journey was on my bucket list for two reasons: I wanted to retrace many of the journeys I had taken with my parents almost sixty years earlier, and I wanted Kristen to see the vastness of this country. It was a trip to remember and savor, and it opened up new vistas for Kristen. One day, as we traversed Minnesota and the miles and miles of absolute nothingness, she turned to me and said, "Mom, I'll never say Delaware is in the middle of nowhere again." We still laugh about that one.

Although Kristen had driven from Connecticut to Florida and on to Dallas, Texas, and even flown to California, she had never really experienced the closeness of driving across country from coast to coast. Watching the scenery flash by, experiencing that vastness firsthand. We had a picnic lunch at the Dunes National Park in Michigan overlooking Lake Michigan, marveled at the hugeness of the Presidents at Mt. Rushmore, and hopped and skipped over ashen gray mounds at the Badlands in South Dakota. We sat at the base of Devil's Tower in Wyoming with our mouths agape in amazement as we watched grown men and women scale the vertical face of it just because it was there.

We arrived in Yellowstone during a raging forest fire across the lake from our lodge and took a boat trip on Lake Yellowstone, where the shore was barely visible through the smoke. We drove through a herd of bison who were bigger than life and ignored our presence from a lifetime of mingling with humanity. We watched a dwindling Old Faithful geyser as a ranger told us her lifetime was limited. We spent far too little time in this natural wonder.

Kristen's favorite park, hands down, was Yosemite, with its mighty glaciers, gigantic redwoods, waterfalls, valleys, and vistas holding out their hands, inviting you to explore them. Overlooking Half Dome on our first afternoon, we witnessed the swearing in of some thirty people who were becoming naturalized citizens. Just remembering it brings tears to my eyes – it was that emotional a ceremony. We could have stayed there forever.

One of our last stops however, was a man-made wonder –

the hot air balloon fiesta in Albuquerque, NM. In one hour, over 300 balloons were launched at daybreak, and we were standing right in the middle of all of them. In the next hour, another 300 were launched. We stood in wonder as the sky was darkened by almost 700 balloons of every size and shape floating overhead. Most were your normal multi-colored balloons, but one looked like Darth Vader, another Elsie the Cow. The Wells Fargo balloon was shaped like a stagecoach. At night, the balloons were all tethered down and inflated to provide a fairy tale glow, followed by fireworks. It was magical. But I believe our most joyous couple of hours during the trip was when Kristen and I took a balloon ride over Albuquerque. We silently glided along and watched the sun rise. So peaceful. So how much I wish our lives could be.

I think that trip ignited in Kristen a love for travel, for National Parks (we stopped at about fourteen, I think), and a love for the diversity of beauty that can be found all over our country. She said to me recently, "Mom, if I am ever alone I'll pack a tent and travel from one park to the next park and paint all day."

I really liked that thought. I hope I can provide her the means to do it.

We pray continually for something to change or for there to be a change from limbo into heaven. Well, there isn't much I can do about any of them except encourage her to continue painting, help her move toward independent living and, should she want to move forward on her reassignment surgery, help her find the resources to do that. I can also provide her with a safe haven, a place where no one will molest her or hurt her. I can provide her with food and clothing. I can help her through the maze of life's practicalities that are difficult for her to grasp. I can shower her with the unconditional love I have always had for her and give her my acceptance and encouragement in whatever she endeavors. I can pray for her health, happiness, and fullness of life. Much as it pains me, however, I cannot give her a life and I cannot guarantee her happiness. Would, dear God, that I could.

And so, here I am in 2017, still in the middle of the muddle of life where I started, in my particular limbo. Waiting. Only God knows when we will enter heaven. What isn't in limbo, however, is Kristen's gender identity. From her birth, she was always Kristen.

EPILOGUE

Just after her forty-seventh birthday, on October 24, 2015, Kristen posted this on her Facebook page. It breaks my heart as I read it, but I think it is an honest, fitting epilogue to leave this where we began: in the middle.

After 15 years of living as woman, I have returned to the place where for me it all began, Provincetown, Massachusetts, and an event called Fantasia Fair. In the beginning, it all seemed to be too good to be true, and it was. Here was a place that seemed to be accepting and allowed a person to be themselves in a real-life situation. But in reality, it is just an illusion of how life and people should treat each other. The reality is people like myself who identify as transgender, transvestite, transsexual or any other gender variant or those who are be-

ing their authentic selves face a world that is all of sudden supposedly accepting of the decisions we make to try and be happy.

The reality of it is that we become accepted kind of like the bearded woman in the freak show. Society accepts us as humans, but only barely. A big part of that is how we as trans people act and present ourselves to the rest of the world and even how we treat others who are struggling with gender identity. If you can pass as a woman, you are regarded as either someone to look up to or someone to hate within our own community. If you can't pass and get read as a man in a dress, then you are relegated to the level of someone who belongs in a circus. And while there are no doubt stories of people who do transition successfully and overcome the labels to live their lives as their chosen gender, I have found in this day and age it is very difficult to be yourself and live a life without discrimination unless you create a new lie and never give up your secret. Maybe a witness protection program for trannies would work.

The new-found exposure and public awareness of transgender people, their fight for acceptance and understanding, is both a welcome change and our worst nightmare. On one hand, we can now get most documentation changed to reflect our outward appearance. On the other hand, it is harder to live a life as the gender we feel is correct. Increased awareness and exposure makes people recognize trans people almost to the point where it becomes impossible to truly live a life as the gender they feel is correct. And if that isn't bad enough, the probability of finding someone who will love you for the person you are becomes so low it seems unattainable.

In the years I have been living as a woman, I have gone from someone who believed I could really be a woman, find someone who would love me as such and be happy, to understanding that no matter how much I wish and hope, there is no true way I will ever be accepted as a genetic woman. And in reality, I have come to accept that I can only come close to what I feel I am. I will never give birth to a child, I have never had my period and I will never be accepted as a woman by either a man or a woman if they know my birth gender. It is what it is and it's a lie if any one tells you differently.

If you doubt what I say, tell someone you had a sex change and see how they treat you or if you ever get invited to a party they are having. And if you are transgender, just think of how many times you have heard someone laughing or heard a couple of women giggling and thought they were laughing at you, because they probably were. Of course, these are just the thoughts of someone who is deeply troubled with their identity and shouldn't be taken seriously because they have issues. I mean how can you take a man in a dress seriously? It's just too funny.

ACKNOWLEDGMENTS

I want to thank my husband for his encouragement, devotion, and editing skills. He probably knows this book by heart after some five or more edits, from a rudimentary draft to this final version. More than anyone else, he lived this journey with me, and survived as a step-dad, when many would have faltered and failed. His love was solid, strong, and enduring even as it continues to this day.

I want to thank my daughter, Kristen. She had less to do with the generation of this book, but she was on my journey, day-by-day, step-by-step, for better or for worse. Most of all, she taught me the power of love amid chaos and confusion, walking with me in unwavering love on those days I wanted to kill her, or me, or both. And who, after reading the manuscript, gave me a big hug and said, "I love you, Mom," when I thought she might want to trash the publication.

I want to thank my editors, Maribeth Fischer, Susan Sutphin,

Ellen Collins, and Crystal Heidel, members of the Rehoboth Beach Writer's Guild, for their strong support and reassurance. They inspired me to keep going, to persevere, and endure. To finish what I'd started too many years ago to count.

I want to thank a small group of folks, straight, cross-dressers, and trans-ladies who read the draft of Always Kristen and provided invaluable feedback.

I want to thank all the classmates in all the RBWG classes I took who listened, critiqued, and spurred me ever onward as I read piece out of context piece of Always Kristen. I could see them trying desperately to follow the storyline, rolling with the switching tenses between past, present, and future, and groaning at all the grammar mistakes everywhere. You are the best.

ABOUT THE AUTHOR

Rita was born in Michigan and spent the early part of her childhood in California. She moved to New York when she was fourteen and later settled in Connecticut with her husband and two children. Rita eventually divorced her first husband and married her soulmate in 1980. After being a stay-at-home mom for almost eighteen years, in 1977, she worked for GE for the next eleven years as an internal management consultant and was a Principal in her own consulting company until 1991. After retiring to Florida, Rita was called to the ordained ministry and attended Virginia Theological Seminary. She was ordained as an Episcopal Priest in 1999. She has served churches in Florida and Delaware. She is currently retired and devoting herself to her writing and her genealogy research.

Rita has had articles published in *Offshore Magazine*, *The Seminary Catalog*, *The AMBO*, and *The Delaware Communion*. During her time at GE, she also wrote several technical manuals on management techniques. From 1993 to 1996, she wrote a column on condominium living for the *Siesta Key Pelican Press* and continues blogging for her condominium development and on her blog, Wordsfromthecrone.com.

She has a BS in Chemistry from Sacred Heart University, an MBA from the University of Connecticut, and a Master's of Divinity degree from Virginia Theological Seminary.

Rita has been a member of many non-profit boards, including the Boys and Girls Club, Inc.; The Claymont Community Center; Primeros Paso, Inc.; The Sarasota Concert Band; and Integrity, an LGBT Support organization. In 2014, the Governor of Delaware appointed her to the Child Placement Review Board.

Rita enjoys reading, writing, genealogy, playing bridge, Scrabble, and traveling with her family. She lives in lower Delaware with her husband, daughter Kristen, and AKC Grand Champion Maltese, Loki.

Made in the USA
Monee, IL
15 December 2019